Praying
Today

Also by Norman Pittenger

Life in Christ
Life as Eucharist

Praying Today
PRACTICAL THOUGHTS ON PRAYER

by
NORMAN PITTENGER

WILLIAM B. EERDMANS
PUBLISHING COMPANY   Grand Rapids, Michigan

Library of Congress Cataloging in Publication Data

Pittenger, William Norman, 1905-
  Praying today: practical thoughts on prayer.

  1. Prayer. I. Title.
BV210.2.P53   248'.3   73-20146
ISBN 0-8028-1566-9

Contents

Preface

Throughout human history men have engaged in prayer. They have addressed themselves to a power or powers greater than human, seeking somehow to enter into communication with the reality upon which their lives depend. They have expressed their gratitude, uttered their petitions for themselves and for others, asked pardon for wrongdoing, endeavored to discern the purpose which that greater than human reality has for them. They have done these things privately and publicly, in their lonely moments and in social gatherings. And throughout *Christian* history, prayer has been conceived as a relationship with the God and Father of Jesus Christ, the God who is the "power greater than human" but who cares for his world and his human children and whose "nature and whose name" (as Wesley put it) "is Love."

But today a very considerable number of people who would profess themselves Christians do not find much meaning in prayer. Or if they do, it is a somewhat stale kind of thing, to be done in church services but with little personal demand upon them. Contact with God: what can this mean for them? Much that they have been taught about prayer, in school or at home or from sermons, does not speak to their condition; they wonder if it really matters at all. For those who do not have faith in God or who subscribe to the idea (much bruited a few years ago) that "God is dead," all this would be natural enough. But for Christian people who *do* have faith in God as the living One, it is very strange.

On the other hand, young people from many different backgrounds seem to be much interested in prayer these days. But they do not consider that the Christian Church has much to say to them on the subject—perhaps with justice, since so often, in Christian circles, prayer has become little more than a formal exercise without deep significance for this or that particular man or woman. So these young people turn to the eastern religions and their methods of meditation, or to some esoteric teacher who tries to show them "how to pray," or they attempt to discover for themselves what prayer may mean and what it may become in their own experience.

I have written this little book with the desire to show all such people, young and old, that prayer is a valid exercise and that it is at the heart of Christian discipleship. As I attempt to demonstrate, prayer is essentially what the old masters of it have said: our conscious and intentional, or attentive, relationship with God—and with God as "pure, unbounded Love," the "Love that will not let me go," and the Love that in Jesus Christ is both portrayed and enacted in the midst of our human history and situation. At the same time I have tried to look at prayer in a new way, by getting at its roots, by relating it to the kind of world we know nowadays to be ours, and by speaking about it in the light of present-day understanding of our selfhood. From one point of view, I have said nothing new: I have only sought to recover emphases known in the past but forgotten by many for a long time. From another point of view, much that I have said *is* new: for to state old things in a new way is often enough to find oneself obliged to say new things too.

For those who are interested in the "case" that can be made for prayer, I may refer to another book of mine, *God's Way with Men* (Judson Press, 1970), in which I discussed the relationship between God and men and argued for the validity of prayer as central in that relationship. In the present book I have spoken only incidentally of the "case" for prayer; my purpose here is to make suggestions about the actual practice of prayer, including the question of its effectiveness, the various kinds of praying in which we may engage, the significant exercise of private prayer and of public prayer, the way in which the Lord's Supper (or Holy Communion or Eucharist—call it what you will) sums up all our praying, and finally the point of prayer in the total context of Christian faith itself.

If the reader is helped to see the importance of prayer, its contemporary possibility, and something of its actual practice, I shall feel rewarded for my labor in writing this book.

Norman Pittenger

1 / Prayer
and the Modern Man and Woman

Many of our contemporaries, including committed Christian people, have difficulty in understanding prayer and an even greater difficulty in seeing how to engage in it. For them prayer is a problem. So much has changed in the world, so many older beliefs and ideas have been abandoned or if not abandoned then gravely doubted, so much of our modern way of living appears to make prayer unintelligible, that they are puzzled about the whole enterprise.

Prayer is not basically a problem to be solved or a question to be answered; it is something to be *done* —older writers spoke of the "*practice* of prayer." But we do not live in a time when Christians can sing, without any doubts or questions, such a hymn as James Montgomery's, written in 1818:

> Prayer is the soul's sincere desire,
>   Unuttered or expressed,
> The motion of a hidden fire
>   That trembles in the breast.

That hymn affirms that "prayer is the Christian's vital breath, the Christian's native air." Perhaps that ought to be the case; most certainly it is not always the case with modern Christian men and women. They are more likely to find appropriate the very last words of Montgomery's hymn, "Lord, teach us how to pray"; and they want to know the why as well as the how of it. In Montgomery's day, people of all Christian communities took for granted the reality of prayer and believed that without prayer Christian life could not be lived nor Christian faith maintained. They may not themselves have prayed often or prayed well; but they accepted prayer as part of their Christian existence. Only a blind observer could say that this acceptance is universal today.

Two hundred years before Montgomery wrote his hymn, George Herbert (the saintly vicar of Bemerton in Wiltshire, England) wrote one of his greatest poems. He piled image upon image to express the importance and reality of prayer. We need quote only the first four lines to remind the reader both of the splendor of Herbert's imagery and the depth of his conviction:

> Prayer, the Church's banquet, angels' age,
>   God's breath in man returning to his birth,
> The soul in paraphrase, heart in pilgrimage,
>   The Christian's plummet sounding heaven and earth.

For the man who wrote those lines and for those who read them it was an obvious fact that a Christian must and did pray. His prayer might be feeble, imperfect, or misguided; doubtless many who recognized its importance neglected its use. Nonetheless, prayer was both right and necessary. It does not seem so to many in our own day.

What is the cause of our contemporary problem about prayer?

I suggest that there is not one cause but a constellation of them. And the problem must first be faced honestly; only then can we go on to consider the how of prayer, its various aspects, its basic meaning, and its relation to Christian life and faith. In this chapter we shall look at some aspects of the problem and in the next chapter we shall seek to offer an understanding of prayer that combines the two essential points of (1) continuity with our Christian past, so that prayer can be seen as an historically validated enterprise, and (2) sufficient relationship with what we now know about the world and ourselves, and how we can now speak meaningfully about God, so that prayer can be practiced without the feeling that he who prays is running away from the real world in which he lives.

First of all, then, there is the *practical* aspect of the problem. It is not enough to say that people are simply indifferent or lazy in this business of praying. On the contrary, many are concerned about the matter and *want* to pray. Let us do them that justice. But the world in which we all live is busy and hurried. It is not easy to find either the occasions or the places where we can be alone. In crowded apartments in housing developments, in the congestion of city life, in the hustle and bustle of daily work, "somebody is always underfoot," as one woman remarked when she lamented the near impossibility of finding the opportunity "to sit down and think for a bit." This situation is so obvious that it need not be spelled out in further detail; it is familiar to most of us all of the time and to all of us much of the time.

Yet we know that when somebody feels that this or that activity is of very great importance, time is made for it and place is found for it. And here we come to the heart of the practical problem in prayer. What seems to be the sheer irrelevance of prayer has so reduced its importance for modern people that they see no reason why they should go to the trouble of making room for it. This is not because they do not care or are indifferent or lazy; it is because they see no practical point in the exercise. They do not recognize the relation of prayer to the exigencies of daily life with its duties and responsibilities. It appears to them to be an escape from the harsh realities of the world, a running away from the responsible concerns that both as human beings *and* as Christians they know to be theirs.

The answer to the practical aspect of the problem moderns find in prayer, then, must be found in a definition of praying that makes sense in and makes sense of our daily life. We need an understanding of prayer that will bring up to date the truth in the ancient Benedictine maxim: *orare est laborare*, "to pray is to work," and its converse, "to work is to pray." Work and prayer go together; waiting upon God and doing our job can never be separated for a Christian. And our way of looking at prayer must stress this association of the two. Hence the next chapter of this book.

A second aspect of the problem is found in the general acceptance of the *modern scientific view of the world*. Many years ago an American theologian wrote a book entitled *Prayer in an Age of Science*. The point he was making remains valid today: ours *is* an "age of science," whether we like it or not. The question is whether in such an age prayer can effect anything. "Does it work?" we may well ask. Now this seems to me an approach to prayer that simply will not do; as we shall be seeing later on, it rests on a mistaken definition of prayer. Nonetheless, the issue remains: Can prayer have any significance in a world such as science portrays to us?

All of us *do* accept that picture, with whatever qualifications or reservations. Nobody can live today as if it were not with him all the time. Biblical Christians are as much involved in this as anybody else, since they spend their working lives in just such a world and simply assume its truth for all practical purposes. This age of science takes it for granted that there is a linkage of cause and effect, that it is improper to speak about "intrusions" into it from outside, and that the sequence of events is an orderly and continuous pattern. The way in which we can bring about changes is through observing the so-called "laws of nature"; this maxim, laid down centuries ago by Francis Bacon, is assumed to be true as a general rule to be applied in particular instances, even by those who firmly believe in the reality of God and his care for the world.

When somebody is sick, we send for the doctor or arrange for a surgical operation: why should we pray about the matter? The remedy for famines is better planning of crops through the science of agronomy: what has prayer to do with it? The way to stop floods is by building dams and controlling the flow of rivers; plagues and epidemics are conquered by more precise knowledge about bacteria and viruses: why pray when through the controls made possible by our knowledge of the cause-and-effect linkage we can do for ourselves as much as can be done? This is how it seems to so many today.

Now, quite apart from a proper definition of prayer itself, there is something else to be said. For the popular picture of how things go in a scientific world, of the sort we have just been presenting, is no longer accepted by the leaders in science. Vast numbers of people think that the fact of a relatively settled order of nature, along with the scientific interpretation of change and the description of the inner dynamics of human personality (and much else as well), has ruled out once and for all genuine novelty and made change nothing more than the reshuffling of bits of matter-in-motion. They do not know that at this very moment scientific thinkers have abandoned that older mechanical picture of nature and have come to see, even to insist, that science does not exhaustively describe the whole range of experience nor everything in the world of nature. Science cannot deal effectively with the appreciation of beauty, the enjoyment of personal relationships, judgments of value as to good and bad; its leaders nowadays are modest in their claims, unlike their ancestors in the last century and the early days of this one. Great scientists are humble before the *mystery* of the world, although they work very hard to solve the specific detailed *problems* (very different from "mystery," since a problem can in principle be solved, while a mystery is simply *there*) that the world presents to them.

Furthermore, the evolutionary perspective, which seemed to threaten all freedom and to exclude a religious interpretation of existence, has turned out to be a blessing, since it has introduced us to the picture of an ongoing process in which novelties *do* appear. Deeper pondering of that process has revealed no machine working automatically but an organism characterized by interpenetration of its several parts, with genuinely new things emerging from time to time, and with a real place for decision by creaturely agents. We shall speak about this at greater length in the next section of this chapter.

At the moment, let us agree that the way to deal

with the scientific problem is not by denunciation of
science as such. Rather, it is by insisting that while
the scientific approach is of inestimable importance
in areas where it is relevant, it is not omnicompetent
nor inclusive of every area of experience. It cannot
deal with ultimate questions of meaning and worth,
nor do most modern scientists claim that it can do
this. Above all, science's own discoveries point to a
world that is much more "open" and "changeable"
than many nonscientists recognize. The "integrative
interpretation" (as it has been styled) found in the
"life sciences" (biology and its related disciplines) is
now coupled with an interrelational view in almost
every area of research. In consequence we have a
description of the world that allows room for decisions made by particular "occasions" or moments—
and these decisions, whether at the conscious level in
man or at lower or nonconscious levels elsewhere,
make a difference. In such a world the validity of
prayer may very well be granted, although *magical*
notions about prayer's working must certainly be
ruled out. But the great masters of prayer have always
protested against popular magical ideas of its efficacy.

Our discussion of science has brought us to the
third aspect of the contemporary problem of prayer.
This has to do with our "overall" vision of things,
with *philosophy.* Here there are two issues that require our consideration. The first has to do with
language and its use; the second is about what used to
be called "metaphysics" or how best to understand
the way things really *go* in the world as a whole.

Probably most of us, most of the time, do not
ponder such questions. But the questions themselves
are inescapable. What kind of language are we using
when we try to address God? Are we talking literal

prose or are we speaking in poetical idiom when we say things about our Christian faith? And how does the world really go? Is it a machine in which nothing novel can appear? Is man, with his urgent desires and yearnings, no more than an irrelevancy, like the smoke that issues from a locomotive but has nothing to do with making the engine operate? Or is the world more like a living organism, where new things can happen and where human existence is related with and plays a significant part in what is going on? Questions like these are indeed inescapable; even if most of us do not spend a great deal of time thinking about them, the implicit, unspoken, assumed answers are determinative of how we think and act.

In respect to language, there is no need any longer to fear the challenge of those who used to be called logical positivists. These philosophers said that no meaning whatever could be attached to expressions that did not have a verifiable scientific reference, demonstrable by observation or experiment, or were not merely tautological—that is, the statement was simply a repetition of itself in other words. Nowadays it is generally recognized that there are other tests for language and that the various different areas of discourse—ethical, aesthetic, religious, for instance—have appropriate kinds of talk that need not be, perhaps ought never to be, scientific in character. So it is possible to speak about God, as well as about duty, truth, goodness, and the like.

It may still be asked, however, whether words taken from ordinary speech, familiar to everybody, can appropriately be applied or addressed to God. Are not such words confined in their reference to temporal and worldly events and experiences? And would it not be better to regard prayer as a simple matter of silence, not including any phrasing of our thoughts, desires, and aspirations in verbal form?

But man is differentiated from other creatures by his capacity for making significant sounds; he is a *talking* animal. And he *thinks* in words, too, for the greater part of the time. Silence is necessary sometimes; it is important and good. Yet even in the silence found in "First Day Meetings" of the Society of Friends or Quakers, what the worshippers are thinking will very likely be verbally grasped although perhaps never vocally expressed—but sometimes such expression does take place and the "sense of the meeting" is often stated in that vocal fashion. The significant point about words used in address to God, as well as in all talk about him, is that they are mental or vocal pointers to the suprahuman reality we name when we say "God." Words can never be adequate containers in this area of experience. Traditionally this point has been made by reference to the "analogical" or "symbolical" character of "God-talk." Such talk naturally derives from human experience, contacts, and situations, since those are *where we are* as men. At the same time, it is evocative, suggestive, allusive, and indicative of that which is more than such human experience, contacts, and situations. It resembles poetry—provided that we remember that genuine poetry is *not* "a pretty lie" but is much truer than prose precisely because it speaks from and speaks to the deepest levels of our experience and awareness. This is true about religious affirmations ("God is Father," "God is 'pure, unbounded Love,' " "God redeems us," etc.); it is equally true about our address to deity in our praying.

The metaphysical question in philosophy has to do with how the world goes. An older metaphysic spoke

about God as so much a supraterrestrial, unconditioned, and unrelated "being" or "ultimate reality"
that it made the world of time and space seem unreal
and unimportant. God's only connection with the
world, in that view, was the logical fact of his having
been its creator or the "ground" of its existence. In
recent years there has been a great revolt against all
such ideas, sometimes to the point of denying that
there is anything other or more than the world. The
earlier idea, in which God was simply alien to the
creation, turned God into a static being, with whom
everything was "already made"; hence prayer could
have no real effect and its practice was nearly impossible—how can one address oneself to self-contained
and self-sufficient being with any hope of being
heard? The later idea, with its denial of anything
beyond this world, made prayer senseless because
there was nobody to address.

Happily, things have changed philosophically. Now
there is the possibility of a different philosophical
attitude, one that takes with utmost seriousness the
evolutionary and processive character of the world
indicated by science, but at the same time affirms the
reality of God as the supreme excellence and perfect
goodness in and above (or more than) the world—in
it, because such excellence and goodness is ceaselessly
operative to further the world's development of potentialities; above it (or more than it), because such
excellence and goodness is unexhaustible, more than
merely creaturely, indefatigable, faithful, unfailing.
And this supreme excellence and perfect goodness is
personalizing in its relations with men. It *makes* us, or
lures us, toward becoming persons, and hence must
itself be personalized, a *he* rather than an *it*. In terms
of such process thinking (about which I have written

in *Process Thought and Christian Faith*, Macmillan, 1968), God is not thought to be simply the absolute, self-existent, unconditioned reality; there is a sense in which these terms are applicable as adverbs qualifying God's essential nature—but that essential nature is God's concrete love, his unfailing relationship with the world, his self-giving and willingness to receive from that world, his openness to "affects" from the world and from what goes on in it. This newer approach, from the side of philosophy, has its intimate connection with Christian religious insight, as we shall see in a minute; what is important at this point is that a God like this, related to his creation and open to its "affect" upon him, is a God to whom we can indeed pray, since he is a personal and personalizing agent whose specific quality is participation in the affairs of the world and in the situation of his human children. Thus prayer is a genuine possibility and the practice of prayer may make a difference both to those who pray and to the continuing creative advance of the world in and under God's purpose of love in its widest conceivable sharing.

This brings us to the last aspect of the contemporary problem of prayer: the *theological* issue. How do we think of God, how do we understand his nature, how do we envisage his way of working in the world? I am convinced that a good deal of talk about prayer is vitiated by the assumption that God is an intolerant, indeed we might say an intolerable, tyrant who must be cajoled rather than addressed; and this is tied in with a picture of his nature or character that is fundamentally unchristian or subchristian, even if many Christian thinkers have fallen victim to it.

We have just now referred to the concept of God as a "tyrant"; we might also have spoken of other false notions of God that have been, and still are, present in the minds of people who profess and call themselves Christians. For example, there is the "imperial Caesar," the dictator who demands tribute from his subjects even if he is benevolently inclined toward them. There is the remote and unconcerned "first cause" or "absolute being," to which reference has already been made earlier in this chapter. Worst of all, perhaps, there is the narrowly moralistic idea, where God is conceived to be the governor of the world who imposes arbitrary laws that must be obeyed or those upon whom they are imposed will suffer ghastly punishment—a picture of God that some sadistic pervert might have thought up, modeling deity after his own character. Alfred North Whitehead, the great Anglo-American philosopher whose thinking is behind the "process conceptuality" to which some of us subscribe, rightly called such ideas idolatrous, and spoke of them as apostasy from the "Galilean vision" (as he styled it) in which God is "modeled" after the figure of Jesus Christ. We can understand how it came about that these false notions were attached to the supreme excellence and perfect goodness "whose nature and whose name is Love." After all, they were prevalent enough among many pagans in earliest Christian times and it was natural for Christian thinkers as well as simple Christian believers to be influenced by them. The tragedy is that they have been allowed a place, for so long a time, in Christian talk and thought. It is time for us to eradicate them and to make absolutely central to all our religious discourse "the God and Father of our Lord Jesus Christ." Here is the clue to "God-talk" if it is to be Christian; as I have argued in my *Love Is the Clue* (Forward Movement, 1968) and *Life in Christ* (Eerdmans, 1972), we have no excuse for perpetuating a picture, or pictures, of God that either make prayer impossible or turn it into an indecent effort to persuade God to be kind to his children.

Talking with ordinary Christian men and women, one discovers that while they do not have the technical competence nor the verbal equipment of the professional theologian, they *do* raise what in fact are genuine theological issues. One of these issues has been put to me in words like these: "Altogether too much teaching about prayer, particularly in circles that are highly orthodox and consider themselves also highly biblical, amounts to telling us that we must cringe before imperial majesty, as if we were in the presence of an oriental despot. What about Jesus' own attitude and teaching? Did he not imply that we were to make, freely and gladly, a response of loving obedience and obedient love to a heavenly Father who purposes the good of his children, who wants them to be free men and not to act like slaves, who works in them and for them so that they may fulfil their possibilities, and who deals with their misdeeds and failures in a loving way and not in condemnatory judgment?" I am convinced that for men and women who feel something like this, prayer becomes impossible or a sham. They can be greatly helped if we affirm, without hesitation and without doubt, that *love* is the key to everything about God. What is more, they can be greatly helped if they see that this is indeed the chief stress in public prayer or church worship, so that such social praying is undertaken by a family of God's children addressing a loving Father (who makes demands upon them, to be sure, but who is no hateful dictator nor absentee ruler nor moral tyrant, but genuinely concerned for their best development as his children), rather than a kind of law-court or imperial audience with a terrifying deity. "God is love; and he that abideth in love abideth in God and God in him"—so the Johannine writer put it. And so ought we to think and act *and pray*, whether in private or in public.

We have now looked at four aspects of contemporary difficulty about prayer: practical, scientific, philosophical, and theological. It is time to move on to a definition of prayer that will be genuinely Christian, in continuity with the past centuries of Christian faith and life, and in relationship with all that we now know about the world and ourselves. What we shall discover, I believe, is that such a definition will not differ very much, if at all, from those put forward in the early days of the Christian fellowship and re-affirmed through succeeding ages by people as different from each other as John of Damascus, Thomas Aquinas, Martin Luther, John Calvin, and John Wesley. But it will not do simply to quote these great Christians and think that the matter is settled. We do not live in their day; we live in our own. That should tell us that we must work our way through to our own way of phrasing the matter. Then we shall find that what we have "invented," in the modern sense of the word (made up or devised), will be very much like what we "invent," in the ancient Latin sense of the word (discover to be already there), although we did not know it and hence had to find it out for ourselves.

Prayer is *not* an attempt to fashion the world after our own desires. It is *not* an effort to coerce the powers that be to do exactly what we think would be right because in conformity with our own ideas of how the world ought to go. It is *not* a denial of whatever regularities or ordering there may be in the created order that scientific research can discover. It is *not* "pestering the deity," as someone has phrased it, so that he will intrude himself into a world from which otherwise he is presumed to be absent. It is *not* a final effort to persuade an unwilling God to do what we find we cannot do for ourselves. Prayer, in the Christian sense, presupposes a creation in which human activities, like every other event or occurrence, have consequences and make a difference. It assumes a world in which God is no absentee ruler but a present agent working "in, through, and under" created agencies—to use a Lutheran phrase originally referring to Christ's presence in the Lord's Supper and the material elements of bread and wine.

The language prayer uses is bound to be figurative, imaginative, and poetic. This is the way we talk in personal relationships one with another; but in prayer the language points toward realities that exceed (although they do not deny) the mundane things with which we are familiar. And prayer is related to this world, with its demands and responsibilities; it is no "flight of the alone to the Alone," as Plotinus put it, but rather it springs from and has to do with man in his inevitable and inescapable involvement in what goes on here and now.

Above all, as we shall see in a moment, *Christian* prayer is addressed to God as "pure, unbounded Love." It is an intentional and willed relationship with what Dante called "the Love that moves the sun and the other stars," faithfully, intimately, unfailingly at work in the world. Prayer is attentive communion with God conceived as this Love, this Lover. And its end or goal is that men and women shall realize and be enabled to express their God-intended

PRAYER AND THE MODERN MAN AND WOMAN   25

potentialities as they are being "made toward the image of God," in cooperation with and sharing in the divine Love.

If this were understood and implemented in concrete practice, it would be recognized as important enough to require that we give time to it. It would bring about drastic revision of much that is said and done in public worship, in hymns, in spoken prayer, and the like. It would have an appeal to our contemporaries, especially among the young who now turn to eastern religions and esoteric cults to find the reality of prayer. It would indeed be known as "the Christian's vital breath," to return to James Montgomery's hymn, precisely because it would be recognized as "*God's* breath in man."

The remainder of this book will be given to further and detailed development of the definition just suggested, to the ways in which we may pray in words and in thought, to the place of prayer in public worship and above all in the Holy Communion or Lord's Supper—which all Christians save the Quakers and the Salvation Army know to be the central act of public worship, however much they may sometimes slight that importance in church practice—and finally to see how it all "fits in"—how faith and action are related to, and find fulfilment in, prayer both private and public.

2/ Coming to Understand What Prayer Is

God is Love; he is the cosmic Lover. Everything else that we say about him, as creator, redeemer, companion, the maker of moral demands, the righteous and just one, must be referred back to that abiding Christian conviction. Otherwise we can hardly claim to live up to the Christian name or pretend to be disciples of the Lord Jesus Christ. And this is as true of prayer as it is of other aspects of Christian life.

The God who is Love is also the God who works unceasingly in the creation. He is related to it in the most intimate manner; as theologians put it, he is immanent in the world as well as more than the world—transcendent. He is incarnate in the world, too, having taken upon himself the reality of manhood and human experience in his Son our Lord Jesus Christ; and elsewhere he also is present in what may rightly be styled "an incarnational manner," since in, with, through, and by creaturely agents he is actively at work there. When we put together the Christian conviction that God is Lover and the fact of his immanent and incarnational activity, we have a picture of a world that is dynamic, moving toward real goals, with genuine continuity in the process yet with new occasions when God's love is signally manifested and operative. Indeed, the world is basically a way in which the supreme Love that is God expresses himself.

Furthermore, this cosmic Love is no *thing;* it is personal and personalizing, since it is a unity in itself, with goals for which it works, with relationships that are more like those we know with each other than like those proper to things, and with the capacity to communicate with men in full awareness and self-awareness. These are the ingredients of personeity (to use a word of Samuel Taylor Coleridge); and that is why we cannot think of God as less than personal, to be conceived not as "It" but as "He," and to be addressed as "Thou."

In that context prayer is to be understood. Otherwise it will be *mis*-understood. But if this is the case, what then is our best definition of prayer? I shall give the one that seems to me to be right; then I shall comment on it.

Prayer is the intentional opening of human lives to, the alignment of human wills with, and the direction of human desiring toward, the cosmic Love that is deepest and highest in the world because it is the main thrust or drive through the world toward sharing and participation in genuine good—and hence toward the truest possible fulfilment of human personality as God wishes it to become. Private prayer is the way we do this in our own particular personal ways. Public prayer or church worship is the way in which we unite with others in expressing dependence on this Love, opening ourselves to it, and willing cooperation with it as "fellow-workers with God."

And prayer at the Lord's Supper or Holy Communion is an identification of those present with the self-offering of Christ to his heavenly Father, as we are nourished by his risen life in the receiving of bread and wine and so "make memorial" of him and of all that he did and was. The end-product of prayer is conformity with God's purposes, joy in his fellowship, newness of life with him and with our brethren, and the recognition that (in Paul's words from Romans) "God works towards a good end, and in every respect, for those who love him." Thus we are enabled to become the personal instruments for his loving concern as it is worked out in the creation, despite the evil and wickedness, the sin and injustice, the pain and anguish, that are obvious to an honest observer. This way of understanding prayer is very different from thinking of it as the effort to plead with God to do the good; above all, it is very different from magical notions of prayer's efficacy, as if we were trying to use charms to rouse him to action. And it is certainly important enough to engage us and encourage us to persist even when praying is not easy or when we do not much feel like carrying on with it.

Think of Jesus in the Garden of Gethsemane, when he prayed, "Not my will but thine be done." *There* is the great example of prayer; and for Christians it should be all-compelling. But we may look also at lesser examples—for instance, Francis of Assisi and his friends praying continually that they might be "instruments" of the "Divine Charity." They asked, in words that have become celebrated in Christian history, that they might be enabled to give "love where there was hatred, pardon where there was injury, joy where there was sadness, light where there was darkness"; that they might seek "not so much to be

consoled as to console, not so much to be understood
as to understand; not so much to be loved as to love."
Those words show how deeply the early Franciscans
had caught the spirit of Christ their Lord and Master;
they show how faithfully they followed the example
of him who "came not to be ministered unto, but to
minister" and whose whole life and death was a
self-offering to God so that God's will might effectively be accomplished in the world.

To some it may seem that the early Franciscans,
and even Jesus himself, are advocating passivity on
the part of those who pray. But the passivity here in
view is neither sloth nor indifference nor some variety
of "do-nothing-ism." It is an *active* passivity. It is the
demanding passivity of those who would be made
"patient" of use by God; and that means a willed
opening of the self so that all one's efforts and
energies are at his disposal. Two things follow. First,
as all who have prayed seriously will agree, the cosmic
Lover is enabled to use the human agent, despite that
agent's failures and defects, for the good that he
would establish. Second, such opening is the way in
which false self-assertion, pride, and the other obsta-
cles to genuine growth as God's child will be over-
come. Like calls to like: the Love that is God
awakens, stimulates, and strengthens the capacity for
loving that is God's very image in his children. One
who has been caught up into the divine Love becomes, through his praying, a participant in the ongoing movement of that Love in the world; he becomes
a lover—and that is what man is being made for, what
he is to become as under God his personality is
integrated and energized and directed.

The best way to come to such an understanding of
prayer is by thinking of the common human experi-

ence of being loved by another and of loving that other in return. This experience may be "low-powered," lacking in intensity of feeling, or it may be accompanied by an enormous passion and a yearning for total self-giving to the other who himself gives totally. Such a variation in quality depends on many factors, not least on the particular psychological and physiological equipment of the lover. Yet if the love is genuine, it involves commitment to the beloved, desire to give and readiness to receive, hopefulness in respect to the enrichment provided in the relationship, and above all a yearning for deepest fellowship with the beloved. In some strange way, the lover is an "I" in contact with a "thou," yet he is also made one with the other so that a true union of lives takes place without the slightest loss or diminishment of the distinction between the two who have become one. It is no accident that the Song of Songs finds its place in canonical Jewish scripture nor that in the New Testament the analogy of marriage or the relationship of bride and bridegroom is used to point to the relationship of God and men. Nor is it accidental that in the writings of great Christian masters of prayer a parallel is drawn between sexual love known on the human level and the divine-human love between God and his children. To this point we shall return.

For the moment, however, let us look at the analogy and recognize that a true human lover wishes with all his heart to fulfil the requirements laid upon him by his beloved. These requirements or demands are not imposed in a coercive manner; often they are not put into words; perhaps they are not vividly in the consciousness of either person. What is in view is the necessity each feels to be his very best, to realize all his possibilities, to obey by his own free and glad decision. Thus the lover is purged from less worthy

ambitions or desires; there is an alignment of himself
with his beloved, and he can say, "Your wish is my
command." Once again, deep speaks to deep, like to
like. And this may not be an easy matter; for real love
includes and requires a certain anguish as the complement to its ecstasy. Thus the Spanish folk saying is
right, "To make love is to declare one's sorrow"—
sorrow for defects and also pain (since the Spanish
word here used is like the Italian equivalent *dolore*,
meaning both sorrow and pain), pain from separation
from the beloved, pain suffered as the self is purified
or purged by love. Love is not all sweetness and light;
it can and it does *hurt*. Common human experience
testifies to this; Christian insight confirms what that
experience knows.

Two corollaries are to be noticed, if what has been
said so far is true. The first corollary is that sharing in
love is the strongest imperative to activity. By this I
mean the desire to do what will be pleasing to the
beloved, thus demonstrating the reality of the relationship. This should not be taken to suggest that
anybody can "earn" love by "doing good deeds" for
the beloved. Love is *always* a gift; it is "of grace, not
of works." What is done is an expression of gratitude
for being loved; the works of love are a thanksgiving
for love. When we apply the analogy to our praying,
we see then that faith (and prayer) and works go
together, but that the former precedes and causes the
latter. Christian prayer always leads to some sort of
doing, even if the doing is not always obvious to
others since it consists in a relationship that is "in
secret" and may not always involve external activity
that the world can see. What is at stake here is "doing
the works of him" that loves us, thereby becoming
"fellow-workers with God."

The second corollary is that in the relationship

between lover and beloved true freedom is found.
The man who does not know love cannot know the
liberty that is given when two have become one in
love; he remains a captive to a false centering of self
upon self. As Martin Luther put it, he is *incurvatus in
se*, twisted in upon himself. But by "falling in love"—
and notice how this suggests that love *happens* to us,
rather than is "earned" by us—the lover is captivated
and captured; he becomes indeed a captive. Here
George Matheson's hymn speaks the truth: "Make me
a captive, Lord; /And *then* shall I be free. . . ." To be
held captive *in* love to God who *is* Love is to know
the freedom *of* love. So the Prayer Book says,
"Whose service is perfect freedom," here harking
back to Augustine's golden Latin phrase, *cui servire
regnare est*, "whom to serve is to reign."

In a world like ours, open to new possibilities and
genuine novelty, prayer as the expression of love
between God and man can accomplish great things.
But it must always be remembered that God acts in
his world persuasively for the most part, and chiefly
so on the human level, rather than coercively or by
violent force. An American poet (F. Bland Tucker)
has translated part of the ancient Christian document
known as the Epistle to Diognetus, using these words:
"He [God] came to win men by good-will, for force
is not of God." Perhaps that is a bit *too* strong, since
in the realm of the inanimate and the impersonal God
does employ power, while everywhere he sets en-
forced limits so that contrast and conflict shall not
become sheer chaos or anarchy. But in dealing with
his human children, God's way is the way of love, in
all its tenderness but with all its strength. For love is
no cheap sentimentality, never making demands, always tolerant of the easy and superficial response of

men. Love wants and love demands the *best*, and that means what is courageously active and indefatigably responsive. Lure, persuasion, invitation, solicitation, appeal, require freely given response. This goes with the freedom-establishing quality of the love-relationship. It is true of the finest human love; it is even more true of the love between God and men. And when the response is given in full freedom, as in genuine prayer, things can happen that otherwise could not happen, since *now* God has at his disposal the desires, willings, yearnings, and energies of his human child.

Prayer, so understood, releases men from fear, turning their necessities into privileges. "There is no fear in love; for perfect love casteth out fear," writes John in his First Letter. Love is expressed in prayer; hence prayer is a way of overcoming human fears and anxieties. Of course much depends on what we mean by "fear." There is a right and proper fear; it is awe or reverence toward God—and love does not cast *that* out, for men must worship and adore, in all reverence and awe, the holy Lover who is God; while true love respects the mystery and wonder in the Other (and also in the human beloved one, too). But John is not talking about such "fear"; he is speaking of the debilitating fear that American idiom describes by the words "being scared." And love *does* cast that out. I remember a small child saying, "A Christian ought never to be scared"; how right she was! And prayer is the way to be delivered from faithless fears and worldly anxieties through "the expulsive power of a new affection," as one writer has phrased it.

In this relationship between God and man, expressed in praying, we are brought to a deepened awareness of "the exceeding sinfulness of sin," since we see ourselves as unworthy, defective, sinful beings

in God's known presence. Our response in loving
obedience is so feeble, so inadequate, so distorted,
that we are ashamed of ourselves. This is why frank
confession of sin is appropriate in the context of
prayer. Yet at that very same moment, the reality of
God's love is sufficiently great to provide reassurance.
We are feeble, but God's love is strong; *we* are inadequate, but God is always unfailingly adequate; *our*
love is distorted, his is pure and perfect. And he
accepts us for what we are to become through his
companionship in grace, even though *now* we are far,
far astray. This is what "justification by grace
through faith" tells us, in quite practical experience.
"Just as I *am*" God receives me, since his "love hath
broken every barrier down"; and he receives me for
what I *may be*, since in fellowship with him my
potentiality for loving response is awakened and empowered and I am enabled, more and more, to say
"Yes" to him.

In all that has been said in this chapter, we have
been giving variations on the theme that Christian
prayer is essentially the opening of the self, intentionally and attentively, to the reality of God as cosmic
Lover. It is not an attempt to get our own way by
invoking deity. Jesus said, "Not *my* will, but *thine* be
done," as he addressed himself to his heavenly Father
and as man prayed to that Father in an hour of trial
and anguish. Prayer is the means by which our desires
and our will are brought to care for what God cares
for, to will what God wills, and to do what God
desires to have done. Thus prayer is human passivity
at its most active, human potentiality brought toward
realization, man's "initial aim" made truly his own
although it was originally given him by God, man's

whole life open to become the personalized instrument for the divine Goodness.

We shall be seeing in the next chapter that this understanding of prayer does not rule out "petition," or asking, both for others and for ourselves. However, it puts such petition in a new context, saving it from the danger of turning into a sort of magical exercise by which we secure, through the use of some formula, what our uncriticized and probably entirely wrong inclinations lead us to want. Asking *is* part of Christian prayer, although by no means the whole of it, as so many seem to assume. The validity of asking is tied in with the plain fact that we are in a world where things go wrong and where we know them to do just this. We cannot nor do we wish to extricate ourselves from such a world, at least if we are Christians; and in any event the world is always with us. What we should desire is to live and work to God's glory, where we are here and now. And prayer as asking or petition helps us to do that, among other things that prayer does.

I believe that the understanding of prayer presented here can make sense to modern men and women. Something more must be said about how it fits in with the world as we know it to be; but before we do this, it is worth observing that our approach to prayer is, as a matter of fact, no new invention. On the contrary it is a reworking of the approach that all the great masters of prayer have taught. The ancient Greek theologian John of Damascus said that prayer is "the elevation of the mind to God." Thomas Aquinas, in the Middle Ages, used the same definition. Perhaps the word "mind" is unfortunate; as we shall suggest in a moment, *all* of a man is or should be

included in that "elevation to God." Other classical
writers have spoken of prayer as "the attentive presence of God"—putting ourselves with attention in the
presence of him who is always with us but is *not* thus
attended to all the time. Augustine Baker, an English
writer of some centuries past, said that prayer is "a
desire and intention to a union of spirit with God."
Martin Luther wrote that our "praying teaches us to
recognize who we are and who God is, and to learn
what we need and where we are to look and find it."
John Calvin spoke of prayer as our desiring what God
desires for us and the world.

Behind all these stands the figure of Jesus himself.
Or rather, *kneels* that figure; for in the Garden of
Gethsemane he knelt in prayer, saying, "Not my will,
but thine be done." It is too bad that we fail so often
to put the stress here on the "be done." Jesus was
identifying himself with God, in urgent desire and
entire surrender, purposing that *through him and
through his death* God's loving will would be accomplished. Here was *active* passivity, as we have described it, not negative or passive passivity. And when
Jesus responded to his disciples' request that he
"teach them to pray," he gave them the prayer we
call "The Lord's Prayer" (and which Roman Catholics, with much insight, call the *Our Father*). Notice,
then, that in the prayer Jesus taught the order of
things is this: first, identification with God, his will,
his kingdom of sovereign love; next, asking for daily
bread or what is needed to make life possible; then,
deliverance from evil and from the test that will be
too much for us; and all of it, as Matthew's gospel
recognizes when it adds the doxology to the simpler
Lukan version, to God's glory—so that the divine will

may be done, and be seen done, "in earth as in heaven."

In concluding this chapter, we shall pick up some of the points that have been mentioned briefly with the promise that they would be discussed later. The first has to do with the way in which man as a sexual being engages in prayer. This may surprise some readers, who would think that it is almost blasphemous to bring prayer and sex together. Their mistake comes from assuming that man is a purely "spiritual" being and that prayer is a purely "spiritual" enterprise. The fact of the matter, however, is that man is *both* body and spirit and that if man prays at all he must pray *as* body and spirit. If this is overlooked or forgotten prayer becomes inhuman, unnatural, and unreal. One of the chief reasons for the neglect of prayer and for the rejection of what was thought to be Christian teaching has been the tendency of Christian people to try to be more spiritual than God himself! After all, God must approve of material things, bodies, and the physical stuff we know so well, since he made and makes them.

One aspect of human nature is our sexuality, largely a matter of physiology but (as we now increasingly understand) involving emotional, psychological, and spiritual qualities as well. Human sexual drives and desires seek union with another human being, in as intimate a way as possible, through the sharing of bodies as well as mental concerns. These desires and drives are good; it is only their distortion or disordering that is evil. This sexuality finds its best expression when genuine love is present. And there is a sexual element in everything that we are or do; the urge toward union, physical and spiritual, is basic to us as the *libido* that drives our existence toward fulfilment in an other. Freud stressed this in recent years, but Augustine spoke about it centuries ago. In our praying we should not seek to trample down this sexuality, as if it were displeasing to God. He made it too. What we can do in prayer is to take our sexual instinct and let it find, for the time being, its center in a love that is utterly demanding and entirely good and which will purify human sexuality and rightly order and pattern it, although it will not destroy it nor remove its urgency and its physical accompaniments. By ordering and directing sexuality, that central aspect of our human nature will become still another channel through which we serve the divine Lover, in and by means of the proximate and creaturely human loving natural for us. Our human loving, with its sexual overtones and its physical expression, can thus be set in the context of a divine-human loving that redeems it from triviality, frustration, and ultimate irrelevance.

Second, much of what has been said so far may seem beyond the reach of most of us most of the time, if not all the time. That is indeed true. We are not yet "made perfect"; we are on our way toward fulfilment in God. What matters is not that we have arrived or failed to arrive, but that we are on our way. The direction in which we are moving is what counts most of all. This is true of every aspect of human life; above all, perhaps, it is true of prayer as an exercise in which we engage. The goal toward which we move is just such an identification with the divine Love as shall make us urgent in every area of our lives to perform the divine will. Some have gone a considerable distance, others have not got so far, some are lagging far behind. Very well, then; that is how things are with us. But God takes account of this, and uses us as and where we are. There is no reason, then, to give up praying because we cannot pray as well as we should like or as well as our friend prays; *our* job is to do our best in the particular moment at which we find ourselves. If we do this we may be confident that we shall be able to move a few steps forward; if we do not continue, we may fall into despair, feel disappointed at our lack of progress, and stop praying altogether—and that would be a tragic mistake.

Here we can find help from some things once said by the French writer Jean de Caussade. He lived in a time when prayer was more generally accepted than it is today, but was perhaps no easier for earnest Christians. This French master wrote that the only place where anyone can pray is in what he styled "the present moment." There, and only there, is where we *are;* there, and only there, can a man find, and be found by, God. So we are to identify ourselves with God's love, and purpose fulfilling his will, in that one possible place, the here and now. Elsewhere de Caussade spoke of "abandonment to divine providence," the way in which God *pro-vides* for, or sees to, our condition exactly where we happen to be. To surrender ("abandon ourselves") to him there is the same as finding him in the "present moment"; it is the acceptance of God's will, which is always love, and the implementing of it as much as we can, in the given time and situation that is ours now. After all, we have no other time, no other place, than that one.

In the ongoing process that is our world, we have our human existence. The world is a concatenation of cause and effect, to be sure; it is also an interrelated process where everything affects and influences everything else. It is a dynamic enterprise whose advance is through the way in which each part, including ourselves as men, seeks fulfilment. Through all of it God, the cosmic Lover, is at work, ceaselessly and inexhaustibly moving it toward the good that is his purpose and which is also the good of each and every part. There is struggle here; and we are called to share in that struggle. Precisely because God is no static or inert "first cause" or "unmoved mover" or "absolute self-contained being," but is sheer Love in action, he delights in our joys and suffers in our anguish. Prayer is our willed "engagement" or identification with God in this great cosmic adventure, our willed linking of our littleness with God's greatness through the opening of our lives to the working of the divine Charity in us and through us and for us.

Thomas Cranmer, the sixteenth-century English divine, translated many ancient Latin prayers for the new English Prayer Book of 1549. In one of these translations he omitted a Latin phrase and spoiled the sense of the prayer. In Latin, the prayer says *amantes te in omnibus et supra omnia*, "loving God *in* all things yet *above* (or more than) all things." Cranmer stupidly dropped the first bit about "loving God in all things"; why, we do not know. It was a great mistake, because we are indeed called to find, and to love, God here in the world where he has willed to be present as well as to love him as that which is more than or beyond the world. God is in the world; or the world is in God—we can put it either way. He is not himself the world; he is *in* it, and it is *in* him, for he is the sovereign and untiring Lover of his creation. A modern hymn writer, Laurence Housman, has put it well, "How can we love thee, holy hidden Being, /If we love not the world which thou hast made?" To love the world, in this sense, is to love God in the world and

to love the world as the creative work of God. Of
course God is "more than" the world. That is how
there can be novelty and change, out of "the dearest
freshness deep down things" (as the poet G. M. Hop-
kins so beautifully phrased it). Isaiah said that God
"always does new things"; but it is equally true that
he is in the old and continuous process too. He
possesses infinite capacity for adaptation and adjust-
ment, but he ever seeks in old and in new the best
good of the creation, always takes it into himself, and
uses what is available for his purposes as his creatures,
by their free decision, put themselves at his disposal.

Prayer, rightly understood, is our identification, by
conscious and intentional and attentive act, with God
the great Lover of men and the world. It includes the
whole man; it takes all there is of him. And it makes
him what he is meant to be: free, whole, integrated,
on the way to true fulfilment as a son of God. In
prayer man is even now sharing in God's kingdom,
where love reigns supreme and where all things find
their joy in mutuality and sharing.

3 / Praying in Words

Through conscious and intentional action and consent, prayer makes possible a working of the divine Charity that otherwise might have been impeded or even prevented. This does not mean that God is "finite"; but it does mean that he wills not to work in spite of us so much as in us and through us, by our own freely made decisions. This is the inevitable corollary of our faith that God is Love and that his activity in the world is primarily in and by love. Too often, alas, this faith has' been obscured if not denied by the introduction into our thought about God of notions that, as we have seen, are more appropriate to imperial Caesar or a despotic tyrant than to the God and Father of our Lord Jesus Christ.

As we turn to the actual practice of prayer, we should observe that there have been two broad main categories into which the great teachers of prayer have divided this enterprise. One is prayer in words, vocal prayer; the other is prayer in thought, often called "mental prayer." In the former, we pray (so to speak) aloud, using words to address God; in the latter, we are not so much concerned to use words as to think about God, his revelation, his will, his character, his relationship with us. The former is more like speaking, the latter more like reflection or meditation—and that word, meditation, has often been used to describe much of "mental prayer."

In this chapter our attention will be focused on vocal prayer, praying in words. Yet it is obvious that the distinction is somewhat arbitrary, since often when we are "*saying*" our prayers a moment may come when words are forgotten and we simply *look* with wonder or *think* with reverence. To try to make *sharp* distinctions would be like asking a lover to provide a neatly divided report indicating in detail the various ways in which he has been with and delighted in his beloved. This would be so highly artificial that it would be absurd. Yet the distinction does have its value; certainly it is convenient at least for purposes of discussion.

Praying with words is commonly taken to include petition and intercession, confession of sin, thanksgiving, and adoration. Praying in thought begins with the sort of reflection that is often styled meditation; and then having begun with a period devoted to meditation, it goes on to contemplation, and may sometimes end in the experience that the great mystics have called "union with God." "Mental" prayer in its first step is relatively easy for anybody; when it comes to the contemplative or mystical stages things are different. A great deal of harm has been done by the suggestion that everybody is really capable of those ranges of contemplative and mystical prayer, since many people find, after much effort, that they cannot engage in them. In any event, the saints have known that "union," in the supreme sense intended by the mystics, is not attained by human effort but is (as they say) always a "gift" of God; while contemplation, in the strictest meaning of that term, is only possible for the few who are called to it—although there is an element of contemplation in all prayer, not least in "vocal" prayer, as we shall see. But meditation is something that we do every day, in secular interests, and the move to *religious* meditation is open to anybody who will take the trouble.

In the area commonly known as "vocal" prayer, we shall find it simplest to begin with petition and intercession. This is because most people seem to think that prayer is *nothing but* "asking"; we might as well start where they are, even if we reject the false idea that petition and intercession are all there is to praying.

Petition has to do with prayer for ourselves and *our* needs; intercession has to do with prayer for others and *their* needs. In both cases, however, the prayer is concerned with that which seems, to the one who is praying, desirable or necessary either to himself or for others. The first thing that we ought to see is that if God is Love, bringing before him desires and needs is not in and of itself wrong. The divine Lover wants his human children to say honestly and frankly what they think and feel, without subterfuge or hypocrisy. That should be taken for granted. The difficulty arises when we assume that the purpose of such frank and honest statement is to coerce God into granting what we believe is thus desirable or necessary. Such a view reduces prayer to magic; it is nothing more than the attempt to conform the world and everything in it to human ideas. Several anthropologists, studying the difference between magic and religion in primitive peoples, have indicated that the latter (religion) is much more an intended conformity of things human with the divine, whereas the former (magic) is the effort, by use of formulae or rites, to bring the divine into conformity with things human. Unhappily, a good deal of petitionary prayer as well as intercession seems to be based on the "magical" premise rather than the "religious" one.

Petitionary and intercessory prayer will usually begin in a rather naive way. The one who is praying will "tell God," as we say, what he thinks he needs or what another needs. But if he is a Christian he will add the proviso that any granting of such requests must be in accordance with God's will as revealed in Jesus Christ. The child soon learns that most petitionary and intercessory prayers are not "answered," as the saying goes. He finds that what he wants is not always what he gets. The stage is then set for him to learn that prayer is not "answered" in the obvious and superficial meaning of that word. What does happen is that the desires and wishes of the praying person are gradually purged of self-centered and selfish elements; he comes slowly to see that he should pray, for his own condition and for others, for "an increase of faith, hope, and charity"—as the Prayer Book collect for Trinity XIV puts it—and in consequence come to conform his own desires and wishes to the ongoing purposes of God. In this given world, the thing most necessary for God's children is a relationship to the divine Love that will bring their own lives to fulfilment, in community with their fellows. That means a growth in the capacity to commit oneself to God's love, which is faith; in the openness to and expectation of great and good things that will augment our relationship to him and to each other, which is hope; and in a self-giving and readiness to receive from others, which is love. Whatever else we may think we require or want is secondary; and the person who is growing in prayer soon comes to understand this. The quotations in the last chapter from the teachers of prayer should have made this plain.

Yet there is nothing wrong in saying what we think, at the moment, would help toward our growth and contribute to the making of our personalities. Not only is there nothing wrong about this; it is a natural thing to do. Nor is it presumptuous on our part. One might even say that God loves us enough to wish us to tell him these things although he also loves us enough to have ordered the world in such a way that many of these things will not be ours because they are not *really* good for us.

The addition that our petition and intercession make to the force for good in the world, once our praying is delivered from sheer selfishness, is very important. It augments the general drive for good; it contributes, as we may dare to say, to the energies of love that are at God's disposal in his ordering of the onward movement of creative advance in the universe. We have already urged that every human decision makes a difference, since it affects all occasions or occurrences—nobody lives "to himself" alone. Hence we should not discount the contribution that our petition or intercession may make. But again, *not* in a magical way. That is, the contribution is the giving of our own desire for good, whether expressed through our personal growth or through the growth of others. Often enough, so far as *others* are concerned, that is *all* we can do. So far as *we* are concerned, the point is that we desire such "growth in grace" as shall make us fit instruments for the divine Love; and in our ignorance or with our limited

knowledge we ask also for whatever may help toward
that end. We learn, then, that the child's prayer for
this or that is harmless; but the adult's prayer must be
childlike, not childish—it will be the acceptance of
God's will, humbly and gladly, as we come to see that
in and through everything "God is working towards a
good end for those that love him." Our immediate
impulse is to want what is *not* for our own good,
harmful perhaps to others, and quite possibly not in
accordance with God's will for good. The developed
type of petition and intercession is more profound; it
is the urgent yearning, expressed in word, that we
shall be what Whitehead called "co-creators" with
God and what Paul styled "fellow-workers" with him.

Intercession is basically the remembering before
God, or the holding before him by conscious intention, of those who are (as we think) in need of his
particular help. When we intercede, we bring others
within the ambit of our own willed relationship to
God; we also add, as we have said, our bit of goodwill
to the cosmic thrust for good in the world. Intercession is not an attempt to *force* God to do something
that otherwise he would not do. To think in this way
is to be faithless, for it suggests that we do not really
believe in and commit ourselves to the Love "that
will not let us" (or anybody else) fall outside the
loving purposes with which he works in his world.

But how can petition or intercession really make
any difference? The answer to this natural question
depends on the sort of world view we entertain. If we
think of everything as "laid on the line," with no
possibility of openness in the creation, obviously it
can make no difference for us to pray in these ways.
On the other hand, if (as we have just said) our
decisions make a difference, if the future is not a

"closed future" but is open even for God, then we can see that there are possibilities that cannot be realized until and unless there is human consent to that realization. Theologically speaking, this entails the view that God is not utterly atemporal, as "eternity" is usually taken to suggest; he is supremely temporal, in that he is in time more deeply than any finite creature could be, knowing possibilities *as* possibilities but not determining them instead of the creature. He waits for and counts on human response; only in this way could he guarantee both the freedom of decision and the responsibility for decision that are an integral element in the created order. If this demands a revision of some popular notions, all the better; our theology at this point could very well undergo a considerable shaking up and a radical rethinking.

All petition and intercession ought to take their rise from actual concrete situations in which people find themselves. It is only when we are wrestling with problems that desperately bother us, only when we are involved with others in such a way that their troubles become our own, that our petitions for ourselves and our intercessions for others can have much reality. Thus prayer of this sort springs from our deep involvement in life, its sorrows, its difficulties, its demand for significant decision. I am going to meet somebody; my petition is that I shall so understand his situation that I shall be able to serve for him as a channel of the divine compassion. I face some overwhelmingly hard decision; my petition is that I shall be enabled so to choose that the divine love may be more effectively released through me. A friend is seriously ill; my intercession is that, in part through my concern for him but more especially through

God's faithful love for him, he may both know and reflect the goodness that through his life can be shown and expressed.

Yet petition and intercession are only the *beginning* of prayer. Even in respect to "vocal" prayer they are but first steps. Hence we must go on to speak of prayer as the confession of our human failings, imperfections, distortions of the divine goodness, and unwillingness to let ourselves be used as channels for that goodness in the decisions we make and the acts we do. The man who thinks that there is nothing wrong with himself or that the human situation is entirely satisfactory will have nothing to confess. But such a man is a very shallow person. He can hardly have looked seriously at himself and he is extremely unobservant of the sadly alienated and estranged condition in which the human race finds itself. Or perhaps he is so self-satisfied and so content with the way things are going that he is unable to recognize what is wrong. He needs confrontation with the love of God in so striking a way that he is forced to judge himself and the situation in terms of that love. Then he will be driven to an examination of his own life and a more serious consideration of the world of human affairs.

Prayer as confession presupposes, then, that there is something to confess. Hence if there is to be any reality in confession there must be an understanding of the self, its wrong decisions and the consequences of those decisions, and the involvement of each of us in the total human situation. This demands that confession should be preceded by some sort of self-examination. Yet here we run into a very serious difficulty, since there is always the danger of becoming overly introspective and of falling into the error of "scrupulosity," against which all masters of the Christian life of discipleship have warned. There can be, often there is, a going over one's past with a "fine-tooth comb," so that all attention is centered on what is wrong and little time is left for the comparison of one's own decisions and actions with the exemplar to which every Christian must turn: Jesus Christ as incarnate Love in action. Furthermore, there is nothing whatever to be said for a groveling attitude before God, as if he were a rigorous moralist or a tyrannical master. Bonhoeffer rightly remarked that some Christian teaching has tried to take man at his worst, even to make him feel worse than he is, simply in order to make him a supposedly receptive hearer of the gospel of forgiveness. Such teaching is worse than perverse; it is definitely and plainly unchristian and should be condemned as such.

Many if not most of our particular sins, as we call them, do not really matter very much. That may seem a startling statement; but what I am trying to say is that the *specific acts* that we do are not nearly so significant as the *main trend* or direction of our whole personality. What we ought to be concerned about in self-examination is not this or that supposed sin—although sometimes these will be obvious and serious enough to require attention—but rather whether we are becoming more open to the Love that is God, more readily concerned to be instruments of that Love, and more willing to share that Love with others, in whatever ways are possible for us in our given place and time. What is the matter with human affairs is that there is an accumulation of wrong decisions and actions that inevitably has produced a state in which right decisions and actions are more and more difficult. This manifests itself in specific sins, of which we need to be aware, both in ourselves and others; but the real problem for us is whether or not we are "growing" toward our intended goal and whether or not society is becoming a more just and fair society.

Any minister who, like the writer, has heard many "confessions" of sin, made formally or informally by parishioners and friends, will be able to testify to the danger just noted. And I hope that many will agree that my own advice to these people is reasonably sound: "Throw away the 'little books' which contain lists of sins about which one should examine oneself. Forget the 'rules,' with all their complications. Instead, look at Jesus Christ. See him on the Cross, loving the world with utter passion. Then ask yourself how *you* measure up to that stark reality." The result of self-examination in *that* fashion will be devastating enough. We shall see clearly how terribly we have failed, how seriously we have shown our lovelessness, how wrong have been our choices time and time again. As Whitehead said, Jesus Christ is the disclosure or revelation of "the divine nature and agency in the world." In the light of that disclosure, we know both how things are intended to go and where *we* have been guilty of failure to cooperate with that "going."

Still another suggestion is to read carefully and prayerfully the thirteenth chapter of First Corinthians or the Beatitudes in the Sermon on the Mount. Having done this, we can then ask ourselves how much of that teaching is reflected in our own decisions and deeds, as well as in the attitudes we take toward others. Again, the result will be searching enough to shame any honest man or woman.

Having done something of this sort, we may then

in our prayer state simply and directly how and where we have been following the wrong path, distorting or denying the creative advance of Love-in-act, and failing to cooperate with others in their efforts to live in accordance with that standard. That is all that is required. There is no need to spend an enormous amount of time in this exercise. An honest confession of this sort ought, for the Christian, to be enough; and when he has finished, he should grasp hold of what the older evangelicals used to call "the gospel promises": the assurance of God's forgiveness that we need. As a matter of fact, the forgiveness of God is prior to our confession of sin. God has already forgiven us even before we have acknowledged our mistakes and defects. It is the confidence that God is Love, hence always forgiving, that awakens in us the sense of our own failure. That is why it is right to begin with the Love that is declared to us in Christ—if God forgives us like that, what must there be in us that needs such forgiveness? That is the right approach, unless the whole Christian faith is a mistake.

One last point needs to be made here. This is to distinguish between "attrition," or emotional anguish over sin, and "contrition," or intention not to continue in sin once recognized as such. Obviously a condition for forgiveness, whether from God or from another man, is that we shall purpose to serve more fully in the future by avoiding those paths which deny love. But God himself has already forgiven us in the confidence, as we may phrase it, that we have a good intention in the future; his forgiveness will awaken that intention, bring it to life, so to speak. There is no need for acute emotional disturbance over wrongs done, although some people may be temperamentally of the sort that feels such disturbance. What matters is the intention to serve God; this is true contrition. And with it goes a forgiving attitude to other persons, for unless we ourselves are ready to forgive we are in no position to receive into ourselves the prevenient forgiveness that God already has extended to us.

We now turn to the two final aspects of "vocal" prayer, thanksgiving and praise or adoration; and we shall discuss them together, as we have just discussed petition and intercession together under one heading.

Both thanksgiving and praise have as their basis the wonder of the divine nature as Love, the ceaseless activity of God in love, and the good things that are made available for men in this world-process where that Love is at work. The two are related, in that God's "nature and property is always to have mercy and to forgive," to labor unceasingly for increase of good in the world, and to receive into himself whatever good is achieved there. Several times already we have quoted Wesley's fine words about "pure, unbounded love": never was there a more apt description of the reality of God, although in Wesley's hymn the words are in fact applied to *Christ*—and appropriately, since in Christ (if Christian faith is right) the "pure, unbounded love" that is seen humanly expressed is the manifestation, reflection, and participation in human terms of the divine Lover whom Jesus called "my Father in heaven."

It has always seemed odd to me that whereas we are often ready to examine ourselves for what we have done or are, we almost never think of examining our lives to see what God has done in them and for us. If we did so, we should find that thanksgiving would be natural and inevitable. Not only "our creation, preservation, and all the blessings of this life"

come ultimately through God's working in the
world—even when they come by way of other men or
from nature, the *chief* (not the *only*, since created
occasions have freedom to be causative agents) causal
agency is the divine Love. But also the sheer marvel
of love, wherever found and enjoyed, above all the
marvel of God himself as Love, provides occasion for
thanksgiving. Many of us hardly seem aware of how
thankful we should be. I recall, however, a true tale
about an old and impoverished woman living in a
mean flat in a slum, who told a visitor that she spent
most of her day in giving thanks to God. "For what?"
the imperceptive visitor asked. And the reply was
simply this, "Because he *is* and because *I am*." A
small child, too, is an example of thankfulness, receiving gladly and responding joyously to what is given
him, even though he has not yet learned to articulate
in words his sense of gratitude. *Ex ore infantium*, the
Latin saying has it; and sometimes, when a young boy
or girl says a heartfelt "Thank you," one sees an
attitude to life that may put an adult to shame.

God is the chief provider, in this sense—which does
not suggest that men are not to provide for one
another, in a society as just as possible and with "fair
shares" all around. But God is also the chief recipient
of all good. What process theologians call "the divine
memory" receives the good that is achieved in the
creation; it counts not only *for* God but *in* God. As
he suffers in our sadness, so he delights and rejoices in
our happiness. All that we do is a contribution made
to God; it is silly, destructive of practical religion, and
denigratory of human existence, to assume that we
cannot *give* anything to God. Classical theology has
sometimes talked as if we could not; but there it has
departed from "working" religion, as well as from

common sense. We *can* give to God ourselves, our
wills, our cooperation, our hearts, as well as whatever
we may do, either singly or as a race, to advance his
purpose of love in the world. And all this is kept and
treasured *and used* by God for further good and
wider sharing in love.

Adoration or praise to God, so closely linked to
thanksgiving, is the highest reach of "vocal" prayer. It
is not something unnatural and difficult, although
occasionally writers on Christian prayer have made it
seem so. But the human analogy of lover and beloved
helps us to see their error. When one deeply loves
another, he wants sometimes simply to be *with* the
other, while sometimes he wants to tell the other how
much he loves him, how much the other means to
him, to praise or adore the other (although doubtless
we do not normally use just those words to say what
we wish to do). From one point of view, an observer
might comment on the absurdity of a lover's doing
this; nothing seems to be "gained" by it and it might
appear just a murmuring of "silly nothings." The
lover knows differently, however. He knows how
natural and right it is for him to do just these things.
So also with the Christian as he thinks about God and
recognizes God's goodness for what it is. There are
long passages in the beautiful book by Ramon Lull
called *The Lover and His Beloved* (which for Lull
meant God the Lover and man the beloved), in which
the beloved simply *adores* the Lover, asking for nothing, wanting nothing, only loving.

Most of us may not be able to reach such an
intensity of devotion; but at least the start of it is
possible for all of us. And it is good for us thus to
adore. We have quoted the Scots theologian Chalmers
who spoke of "the expulsive power of a new affec-

tion" as a means of purifying and ennobling human existence; and the historian of French spirituality, Henri Bremond, has written about the way in which prayer, at its best, is "a purification of the self." Nowhere is this so clearly seen as in adoration and praise. It extraverts us; it focuses our attention on a reality outside ourselves; it liberates us from the mire of self-concern that so often impedes our making any progress in discipleship.

A friend once remarked to me that he could not understand the business of adoration since to him it suggested that God enjoyed being lauded—and such a picture of God, he said, was unpleasant and must be untrue. To which the reply was only this: "Doubtless God himself does not 'enjoy' continual praise, but he 'puts up with it' because he knows it is good for his human children." Yet I could have said more that would have been much to the point: "If God really *is* a Lover, he must delight in having those whom he loves respond to him in love and want to be with him and tell him their love." Is this reply too anthropomorphic, too much a making of God after our human image? I think not, for the simple reason that it is *we* who are "made in the image of God," as Genesis puts it, *we* who are being created to become lovers of our fellow men and of God himself. Therefore it is proper to use that image of love-in-the-making when we think of God himself.

Sometimes theologians and philosophers spend their time either "paying God metaphysical compliments," as Whitehead once phrased it, or in assuming that for his greater glory they must make him utterly alien to everything that we know and experience and care for. But *Jesus* did not take that line at all; *he* used quite ordinary human analogies, drew upon quite humdrum and common human experiences, and called God by the most human of loved names, "Father"—*Abba*, which some experts tell us can be translated "Dad" or "Papa." Need a Christian try to be more "spiritual," more "heavenly," or more cautious in speech, than he whom we call our Lord and Master?

4

Praying in Thought

The distinction between "vocal" and "mental" prayer often seems rather forced and artificial. This has already been remarked upon, although we have been prepared to use the distinction as a matter of convenience. Yet a good deal of adoration or praise, about which we spoke at the end of the last chapter, is entirely "without words"—and thus might very well have been included under the category of "mental" prayer. For by "mental" prayer traditional writers have intended to denote the kind of conscious relationship with God that does not require the use of words, spoken or formed. *Ideas*, thoughts, as well as deeper emotional or "affective" states, are included in this category where the classical writers would place meditation, contemplation, and the various stages of "union with God" about which the mystics have given us reports.

However we may feel about adoration and praise, including it in "vocal" prayer or letting it serve as a kind of borderline approach to "mental" prayer, it is obvious that when we come to meditation we are concerned with a kind of exercise that can quite readily be carried on with no verbal articulation as such.

One of the difficulties many people find in reading about meditation is the variety of "systems" that are suggested to them. There are the Sulpician and the Ignatian and several other "methods"; in each of these it is taught that one proceeds from "point" to "point," moving almost automatically along a line that is regarded as appropriate to the chosen "system." The beginner wonders which "method" he is to choose. He may also think that the very complicated series of steps that the experts propose are not for him—maybe the very holy can follow this procedure but the ordinary man or woman has neither the time nor the interest to do so. In fact, in my judgment, the ordinary person is right. Someone has said that it would have been better if those who worked out these "systems" had never been born; and that comment has its point. Yet it must be acknowledged that sometimes, for some people, the "system" approach has worked and does work; therefore it cannot be entirely dismissed. For our purpose here, however, we shall simply disregard it and consider the simplest and easiest of all ways of meditation, call it by what name one may prefer.

Suppose that you are planning a holiday trip. Obviously you will secure the literature that is relevant. You will read it through, try to discover the shortest route to your chosen resort or the route that has most interest for a person like yourself. Then you will think about the activities in which you will engage while you are there. A great deal of attention is required and you will be quite prepared to spend a considerable period of time in thinking through the whole trip. Doubtless after completing your reading you will sit down and think over your plans very carefully. Now what you have really been doing is engaging in a meditation on your holiday, although you would not have called it that.

Or again, suppose that you have had the privilege of meeting a distinguished visitor to your town. You have been introduced to him, you have talked with him, you may have heard him give a lecture and then answer questions. Now you wish to think over your experience and see what it really meant to you. So you sit quietly for a few minutes and do just this. Again, you have been meditating, even if such a description would not have occurred to you.

Best of all, suppose that somebody you love very deeply has written you a letter in which he speaks of what he has lately been doing, of how much he misses you, of things that you have done together and may again be able to do. He closes with a renewed expression of his love for you and signs with the name by which you call him. After reading the letter it is likely that you will think about this person, think about the relationship between you, and thus find your affection renewed and strengthened. You will have been engaging in meditation, despite the fact that such a word would not have occurred to you. Probably you would say simply, if asked what you had been doing, "Thinking about my dear friend John."

Now meditation as an exercise in prayer is no different from this sort of natural and normal human experience, except that it is thought about God, about God's character and his activity in the world. As an old teacher once said to me, "Meditation is just prayerful and careful thinking about something or someone very important to us."

One begins with some passage from the Bible or

another bit of writing that will be suggestive and stimulating. One reads attentively, in order to get the full benefit of the passage. Then one closes the book and thinks. That is all that is necessary. Sometimes it is helpful in one's thinking to try to picture a scene— for example, Jesus with his disciples in some particular situation that a gospel passage narrates. This "composition" may be of value because it will make vivid and clear what was going on in what has been read. Then one asks, "What does this *mean?*" That is, what was the point of the incident so far as the original participants were concerned? One thinks about what was conveyed to them by the given happening; and one goes on to think about what is conveyed to oneself *now.* "What does this mean *to me?*" one may ask. Then, at the end, it will be appropriate to ask a further question, "If that is what it meant then and what it means now to me, what does it teach me or what does it require me to do?"

Meditation is just as simple as that. It is the intentional, yet not coerced, effort to read or think about, to read *and* think about, some significant incident in God's way with men as reported in Scripture or in some other piece of writing. It may even be thinking about some moment in one's own experience in which one has felt the reality of God or thought that some demand is given or some vision is disclosed. One lets his mind play upon the material until it speaks significantly and helpfully. And then one determines to use in the future the new insight or suggestion that has emerged.

In past ages some of our Protestant forebears did just this with the Bible every night. Robert Burns has a telling picture of such a nightly experience in his poem about the Scots peasant on Saturday, preparing for the observance of the next day as the time for worship and rest: *The Cotter's Saturday Night*. A great deal of the strength of the evangelical Christian's life was derived from a meditative reading of Scripture in this way. In Catholic circles, the believer may not have been so likely to use lengthy passages in the Bible in this way; perhaps he was content to take a very *brief* passage, maybe only a verse or so, and meditate upon it, or even to use a passage from the Fathers of the Church or some "spiritual classic." But the same result followed.

So far as the Bible is concerned, we may notice that it may be read in various ways. Some may wish to use it as an historical book; after all, it *is* a collection of writings bound up together in one volume, telling us of the way in which the Jewish people came by God's self-disclosure to a deeper understanding of the God they worshipped and a more adequate conception of his purpose for his "chosen" race. It leads into the story of Jesus and the results of his coming. For a student of the history of the human race it is an invaluable book. It can be read for that purpose. Then there are the scholars who read the Bible in order to discover the specific relationship of section to section, idea to idea, etc. They may devote their time to textual problems or to other questions that happen to interest them. But the ordinary Christian generally reads the Bible for what he is likely to call the "inspiration" he receives from it. There are some people who decry such a use of Scripture, but I believe they are wrong in so doing. Bible reading *can* provide "inspiration"; that is, it can quicken our minds, warm our hearts, strengthen our wills, purify our desires—and this is all to the good. Yet it is possible today to combine these several approaches in a fashion that can make the reading of the Bible much richer and more rewarding. The use of a commentary discussing the passage that we hope to read can do a great deal to enlighten us about what it has to tell us. Such a commentary need not be technical nor burdened with critical *apparatus;* it may be simple and straightforward, based on scholarly study but not thrusting such study before us. To mention some commentaries that are of this sort, there are the studies by William Barclay, now readily available in paperback form, and there are Mowbray's *Mini-Commentaries* as well as the SCM and the Tyndale series. Anybody who uses these or similar books will be able to read the Bible more intelligently and will discover that the "inspiration" contained in its several parts becomes all the more compelling.

There is always a danger that the Bible will be read mechanically, without imagination. To read it in that way is to miss its deepest message. Even in earliest days, the Church distinguished among what were known as the "senses" of Scripture. There was the straight literal "sense" of a passage, with its presumably historical basis. But there were also the allegorical, moral, typological, "topological" (or spiritual), and mystical "senses." Sometimes the distinctions were rather artificially drawn; yet their point is clear—ancient Christian thinkers knew that the Bible could be read in different ways and for different purposes. Above all, they knew that the Bible should be read with all the imaginative insight one can manage. And in a way meditation on biblical material is just that: after all the other "senses" have been exhausted, there is the imaginative approach that will make it possible for the reader to grasp the *big* meaning of what he is reading.

So much, then, for meditation and meditative reading of the Bible. We now consider contemplation. That word has been used in a variety of ways by the great writers on prayer; but our interest is only in its main intention, which is easy to grasp. Contemplation essentially is wordless looking. A French peasant was asked what he was doing when he sat quietly in church gazing steadfastly at a crucifix. He answered, "I look at him and he looks at me." That was contemplation in its simplest but also most profound sense. *Looking*—but that requires something to look *at*. Otherwise there may only be wool-gathering, meandering thoughts, without any concentration of attention.

It is just here that the Christian faith can speak in a peculiarly effective way. For the center of that faith is not something but *Someone* at whom we may look. Christians believe that in the Man Jesus there is a placarding before men of the reality of God's character, his love, and his action in the world. He is the focus of an unending, manifold, yet faithful movement of the divine Lover in and to his creation. To look at *him* is to look at an action of God. The French peasant *looked at the crucifix*, the symbol Christian faith has hallowed as the best insight we know into the heart of deity. Thus one meaning of contemplation is simply looking at Jesus. The incarnation of God in a human life provides us with a focus for contemplation; and a very large part of Christian discipleship is in looking at that human life as we know it from the gospels or see it portrayed in paintings or statues or in stained glass. There is absolutely nothing wrong with this, even if some have thought that it tended to "limit" deity and made devotion too much centered on his manward activity.

In the story of Jesus we have "Truth embodied in a tale," as Tennyson puts it in *In Memoriam;* and for most of us it is best to concentrate on *that*, knowing that what a French teacher of prayer once said will come true: "Through the wounds of his humanity we will be brought to the intimacy of his divinity." It is possible to become altogether too sophisticated about these matters; I wish to plead for simplicity and availability in the practice of prayer; and I believe that in the incarnate Lord, God has graciously given us just such a simple and available object for our contemplation.

On the other hand, there may be those who can come to contemplate what the mystical writers have styled "the stark vision of God in himself." If by this is meant God apart from and without relationship to his world, such writers have departed from the deepest meaning of the Christian faith and perhaps from the realm of human possibility altogether. But if they have meant that there are some persons who can contemplate deity without the use of any particular set of images or symbols, they may have spoken the truth. For the ordinary Christian who wishes to pray, however, it is likely that this is "too high"; he "cannot attain unto it." In that case he should not *try*. The contemplative who *can* attain to this "stark vision" is very rare. Few of us are John of the Cross or Theresa or Meister Eckhart, who evidently *could* see God thus. Still it is worth observing that when these mystics sought to write about their experience they were obliged to use symbols and images. One thinks of Theresa with her comparison of the life of prayer to a medieval castle, of John of the Cross with his lovely story of the lover in the garden of cypresses, and of Meister Eckhart (the most abstract of them all) with his talk about a spark of deity that seems to become the very self of the person praying.

Such names as these bring us to the mystical "union of the soul with God," as this supreme experience in prayer has been described. But about that we shall not write. There are plenty of books—for English-speaking readers chiefly such studies as those by Evelyn Underhill, W. R. Inge, and Baron F. von Hügel, found in many libraries—that may be consulted. The reason for not discussing this subject, nor indeed the whole range of "mystical prayer," is that in my judgment a great deal of harm has been done by the suggestion that every Christian may advance to mystical prayer if only he will make the effort. I believe this is not the case; as was pointed out earlier, the mystics are few although they are also very important. In a small volume intended to help ordinary people, who most certainly are hardly likely to become "mystics" in the technical sense, it would only be troubling and confusing to deal with such matters. In any event, the writer himself is not a "mystic"; and whatever I might say would be so much at second hand that it could be of little help to others.

The remainder of this chapter, therefore, will be devoted to some topics that are important for any learner in prayer. When to pray and where to pray, for example, require attention. So does the increasingly commended business of "arrow prayers," as they have been called. And something should be said about the use of the old set services of the Church—for Lutherans and Episcopalians that means the reading of Morning and Evening Prayer, or Matins and Evensong. The next few pages will consider each of these topics in turn.

When to pray? That is a question each of us must answer for himself. Years ago it was said that one should pray morning and evening, setting aside perhaps ten or fifteen minutes for the purpose. Once a week, we were told, we should make time for meditation. But such a system seems very difficult for many people in the crowded and hurried condition of life today. All one can do is suggest that immediately upon getting up in the morning, while dressing or (for a man) while shaving, it is perfectly possible to *say* some appropriate prayers of aspiration and self-commitment for the day. In the evening, before going to bed, a short period may be found for further prayers, including intercessions for others and a simple statement of one's own apparent desires and needs, but for the most part a quick confession of failure, a word or two of thanksgiving, and a silent moment in which one praises God for what he is and for what he does. If this is done *daily*, one may be able to arrange once a week a rather longer period of time when one can follow pretty much the full round of petition-intercession, confession (with a brief look at oneself), thanksgiving, praise—and then, at another time, find opportunity for a careful, prayerful reading of a piece of Scripture with five or ten minutes of meditative thought about it. But there is another type of prayer—the "arrow prayer"—that can be said anywhere and everywhere; to it we shall return.

In an older day one's bedroom, sometimes equipped with a prie-dieu at which to kneel, was recommended. Nowadays this is not so readily available for the purpose, except in those houses where each member of the family can be sure of quiet in a room of his own. Thus it may be better to say one's morning prayer of aspiration and commitment in the

way already suggested—while dressing and preparing
to "come down to breakfast." Evening prayers can
very well be said just before going to bed, even in bed
if this is necessary. It is certainly helpful to us,
embodied creatures as we are, to kneel—posture can
make a difference in the attitude we take, to our
"frame of mind," as we say. But it is not of over-
whelming importance in the hurly-burly of contemporary life. Nowadays many churches are open all
day; it would be a wise plan for the rest of us to
adopt the common practice of Roman Catholics and
drop in at a church on the way to work or coming
back from work. It need be only for a few moments,
but the atmosphere is right, especially if the church is
the sort of place that obviously has been much
prayed in. T. S. Eliot in *Four Quartets* speaks of
Little Gidding as a place "where prayer has been
valid"; there are churches like that, too.

What now about the practice we have called
"arrow prayers"?

An "arrow prayer" is a very simple and direct
petition or word of thanksgiving and praise, which
may be said at any time and in any place. Texts from
well-loved portions of Scripture may be selected; one
may find appropriate words in some other book; or
one may make them up for himself. Typical arrow
prayers would be: "My God I love thee; make me
love thee more." "Thank God for life and friends, for
work and fun, for everything." "Help me, O Lord, to
see thee and serve thee wherever I am." The possibilities are beyond number. And one can also pray in this
fashion before undertaking some job, "May I do this
work as well as I can and in a way pleasing to thee"
or "Help me, Lord, in talking to this person who
needs my counsel" or "Strengthen me to face this
ordeal." It is as simple as that.

Related to arrow prayer is the repetition from time to time of some familiar hallowed form of words, trying to make these come alive in one's mind. The Russian Christians often use what is styled the "Jesus prayer." It runs like this, "Jesus Christ, Son of the living God, have mercy upon me"—and it is said over and over again. Is this "meaningless repetition"? Not at all; rather, it is a help to fix attention on the reality of God in Christ, who is everywhere present but to whom we must turn consciously and attentively from time to time if that reality is to be vivid to us.

For many the use of the set services of the Christian Church, as found in the traditional prayer books, can be of great value. Episcopalians and Lutherans are familiar with morning and evening services, called Matins or Morning Prayer, Evensong or Vespers. Those who decide to use these services in private will discover in them a great richness, including Bible selections and Psalms, ancient canticles or songs of praise, prayers that have been valued by millions down the centuries, and above all the sense of taking part in a continuing round of prayer that has given these services the traditional name of *Opus Dei*, "Work of, or for, God."

Finally, it ought to be clear that nobody can engage in prayer "to order." Each of us has his own way, his own *attrait* to God, as the French put it—his particular kind of approach. Therefore each of us should try to work out for himself how he is to engage in prayer. This is true in respect to time and place, in respect to types of prayer—in word or in thought—in which to exert himself; it is also true in respect to rule or plan for church attendance and for receiving the sacrament of the Lord's Supper. We can learn from others; and we should have the humility to want to do so. But in the last resort *we* are the ones who are praying, not somebody else. In any event, one thing is clear. Our praying, whether in word or thought, whether in church or at home, whether at ordinary services in church or at the Lord's Supper, should be grounded in two matters of supreme importance: the reality of God as Love and the concrete place where we happen to be as human beings.

We shall probably never be very good in praying, but that is simply a fact of our feeble, sinful, finite human nature. On the other hand, we must try to be as good as we can—faithful in prayer, persistent in praying, committing ourselves always to God who knows us better than we do and who yet accepts us, and loves us, because we are his "dear children." With this sort of approach, we shall find that our praying is increasingly meaningful, strengthening, and worthwhile. There is no reason for us ever to feel discouraged about it.

5 /
/ Praying in Church

No man lives entirely of and unto himself. He belongs to human society; he is basically a "social being," as the ancient Greek thinker Aristotle put it. This is as true of man in his religious life as in the other areas of his existence. That is why public prayer, or prayer in church (as we who are Christians would put it), is so important for him.

Unquestionably there is a profound sense in which each man's religion is his own, of course. Until and unless faith is deeply personalized and religious practice an equally personal matter, both will be largely superficial and conventional. This is why unthinking acceptance of membership in a religious group can be dangerous; it can produce—although membership as such need not produce—large numbers of people who give nominal assent yet never really enter into the life of the group in any genuine depth. On the other hand, a purely individualistic religion can be equally dangerous, as a celebrated remark by the British economist R. H. Tawney indicates. Tawney said that the man who "seeks God apart from his brethren is likely not to find God, but rather the devil, whose face will bear a surprising resemblance to his own." That is, unless we broaden our perspective and correct our idiosyncrasies by sharing with our human brethren, we are in peril of conceiving God simply as ourselves writ large, with all our peculiarities, self-centeredness, and imperfection.

Sometimes defenders of entirely individualistic religion quote a sentence from Whitehead in *Religion in the Making:* "Religion is what a man does with his solitariness." On the other hand, defenders of the social nature of religion assume that because Whitehead said this he must have been mistaken in his understanding of what religion is. Thus he is attacked from both sides; but both attacks are in error since they fail to read that sentence, and one or two similar ones, in their proper context. The point of his remark is in fact similar to our own comment above. A religion that is never truly made personal, speaking to the inner depths of man's being, will be superficial or conventional and will have no cutting edge. Personal acceptance, personal faith, and personal responsibility are essential; and this is what is mean by the "solitariness" in which a man faces God, the world, and himself with utter honesty and tries to come to terms with all three. At the same time Whitehead saw, and said in that very book, that the "topic" of religion is the individual in the community.

Each of us knows his "solitariness" well enough. Matthew Arnold spoke of the "unplumbed, salt, estranging sea" that divides us even from those we know and love best. Our human need is not to deny this distinction of persons but to find ways in which our social nature can find healthy expression. Nobody is content to live in utter isolation from others, even if this were possible; we want our fellow men, to be united with them in a relationship that preserves distinctions but overcomes separation. And in our religion, we have a *social* reality that is to be *personally* appropriated. This is because of the sort of world in which we live, one where everything is profoundly interrelated, as we have already insisted. The world is not a great heap of individuals closed in on themselves; it is a shared enterprise in which each is open to others.

And that truth about the world rests on the nature of God himself. The history of religion is the story of the purification of concepts of God, from barbaric notions to a picture of him as good, loving, and caring. God is social, too, in that he shares with others who are his creatures; he is intimately related with them, rejoicing in their happiness and suffering with them in their anguish. He not only gives to them; he is also ready to receive from them. Otherwise the creation would be pointless.

Now, specifically Christian faith confirms and validates all this. In that faith God is affirmed to be Love; and by its very definition love means relationships, influencing and being influenced, affecting and being affected, or in a word, sharing. God is always God, but he is not to be thought of as *separated* from his creatures, however distinct from them he must be; on the contrary, his Godhead is declared precisely in his active love in the world. Among the purposes for the coming of Christ, one was to make this divine sharing a vivid and wonderfully real matter for God's children.

Like everything else, the Christian community of faith is a living social process that moves down the centuries, handing on its faith from generation to generation. Its life is communitarian, as we might put it. In another book (*Life in Christ*, Eerdmans, 1972) I sought to make this clear and to show how being a Christian *is* being "in Christ" and hence being with the brethren "in Love" as well as "in love": first, Love with a capital "L" because it is life with God in Christ; then, love with a small "l" because it is life with our fellow-Christians and in principle at least with all men everywhere.

If this be true, then public worship is an elementary duty for all who profess the Christian name. So by a long route we have arrived at the subject of this chapter. It was helpful to take that long route, however, since walking it will have demonstrated that church worship is no incidental matter for the Christian, but rather is grounded in his very human nature itself as well as in his distinctively Christian faith.

Those who talk as if public worship were just an addendum, to be engaged in when we happen to feel like it, have seriously misunderstood themselves and also mistaken the nature of the Christian enterprise. For the truth is that Christianity is incurably a "liturgical" as well as a personal affair.

The word "liturgy" is the ancient term to describe public worship of any sort, although sometimes its meaning has been restricted to the Lord's Supper. Such a restriction is an error, however; the Greek word from which "liturgy" comes is defined in the lexicon as meaning "a public work"—and *all* corporate worship is such a public work. Unquestionably the Holy Communion is, or ought to be, central to Christian worship; so it has been historically, even if (for example) the intention of the great Reformers, Martin Luther and John Calvin, that it should be celebrated each Lord's Day has been observed by many only in the breach. The next chapter will be

devoted to a discussion of that sacramental observance as a focus for Christian public praying. In this
chapter we are concerned with the significance of *all*
public worship as such and with why praying in
church should be part of the normal Christian disci-
pline of life.

The Christian who "goes to church," as the phrase
has it, is doing this as a human being like anyone else.
That is to say, he goes as a body-mind complex, not
just as a "spiritual being." What goes on in his body
affects what goes on in his mind; and *vice versa.*
Further, he goes as one who is intimately related to
his fellows as a social being; with those others he is
"knit together in a bundle of life," as the Old Testament tells us. He is also in relationship to the world
of nature, from which he has been produced through
the purpose and act of God; he is not a stranger in the
natural order, but genuinely a part of it, although as
human he is also distinct from it. Finally, like all men
he is related to God himself, the supreme creative
Lover who is present throughout the creation.

Obviously John Jones and Mary Smith, as they go
to church on a Sunday morning, are not likely to be
vividly conscious of all this. Yet all this is true of
them. They are more likely to be aware of the drive
in them to share in fellowship with others, for probably they are married, have children, have friends and
neighbors, and want to be associated with all these in
varying degrees of intimacy. The physiological-
psychological basis for this urge to share in such
fellowship is their human sexual nature, although this
does not suggest that actual sexual contacts are involved. But we need to recognize this pervasive sexuality in man, as we have argued earlier and shall state
again; nor need we be ashamed of the fact.

When a Christian goes to church, then, he goes bringing with him all that he is as a man, as well as all that he is as a Christian. And the public worship of the Church, in which he is to take part, must somehow be relevant to all these aspects of human existence. When John Jones is in church, his mind is there so that he can understand what is going on. His senses are there so that he will feel, see, hear, touch. His body is there, as he sits or stands or kneels. His sexuality is there, as he learns to care for and respond to his brethren in Christian love. His social relationships are there, since he is with other men and women. His relationship to the natural order is there, because he is the product of it and carries it with him; his spirit, or capacity for openness to God as well as to men, is there too. The public worship of God is a supreme instance of the whole man bringing his whole personality into the open, in an intentional and willed identification with the God whom he comes to worship. When we forget this and focus attention on but one aspect—perhaps on the spiritual side alone—we deny our total God-given nature as men. No wonder that worship can then seem something apart from life, an occasional exercise of extrication from our human situation. But that ought never to be the case.

It is necessary, therefore, that what goes on in church worship should appeal to the whole man and should include the whole man. It should *express* his wholeness, since it is the Christian vocation to offer one's totality to God, as did Christ himself. It should also *impress* him in his wholeness, since as we all know it is through the impact upon us of words, actions, sensed or felt realities, that we come to understand and appreciate. One reason for the unattractiveness of church worship in so many places and on so many occasions is that this appeal to and expression of human wholeness has been neglected or forgotten. The public worship of God ought not to be *just* sermon, important as that is; if *only* the sermon counts, we might as well be in a lecture hall. The setting of the sermon in the context of the total act of worship is what gives the sermon its peculiar significance. It is then recognized and accepted as the proclamation of the gospel of Christ to the people of Christ, gathered to bring all of themselves into responsive acceptance of what God has done for them in the Lord and Saviour whom they would adore and follow.

This is why certain postures—sitting, standing, kneeling—have their place. It also explains why we have prayers said by minister and people, hymns that are sung, movement from place to place in the church building for particular purposes, like the taking of the collection, or other necessary actions. It tells us why we have flowers on the Lord's Table or near the pulpit and why in many churches those who minister—both the ordained leader and the choir, for example—may wear a distinctive garb. In all these ways, a setting is provided that both expresses and impresses—and that is necessary for more than aesthetic motives. Beauty is of great importance in worship as elsewhere in life; in church services, these things have a point that includes but goes beyond sheer beauty, since they have as their principal reason the provision of a context in which the worshippers as whole men and women are moved to pray, to adore God, to listen to his Word, to confess their sin, to receive assurance of his forgiveness, and to be strengthened for discipleship.

There is no excuse for the drabness so often found in church services. It is possible to worship God anywhere; and even the ugliest building and the dullest sermon, the most sentimental or cheap music, the sheer boredom that may accompany the rest of the service, need not block our public approach to the throne of mercy. But it is shameful when lack of imagination, failure of insight, and narrowness of mind produce such a parody of what might well be the most glorious of human occasions of meeting: the worship of God the "altogether lovely" (as an old phrase has it) and the altogether loving One.

Furthermore, we need to do everything in our power to make our praying together in church an occasion in which genuine Christianity is visibly placarded before those who are present. Sometimes the service suggests a God who is like an oriental monarch demanding that his subjects cringe in fear before him; more often, at least in many American churches, it suggests a God who is foolishly sentimental and entirely undemanding in his loving self-disclosure to men. In either case, the worship is less than Christian. In the former sort, the necessity for awe and reverence has been turned into groveling in fear and feeling a hatred of self, neither of which is appropriate when we are intentionally thinking of our austere but loving God who does not want us to hate our true selves (although we ought to hate our lower sinful selves) but to let them be open to him and his grace. In the latter sort, the recognition of God's loving mercy has been turned into cheap "easiness" in his presence; then God is a "soft" God, the sternness of whose loving requirements and the sinfulness of man before him having been forgotten. For my own part, I believe that the first condition for such a revision of our services of worship as shall make them fully Christian is theological; by this I mean that only when our doctrine of God is soundly Christian will these services be appropriate to the worship of the community that finds its center in Jesus Christ, who revealed God as "pure, unbounded Love" but who also revealed that this Love is *not* soft or sentimental—the fact of Calvary makes that truth sufficiently plain.

Some of our comments have been highly critical of public worship as frequently found. But nonetheless, attendance at that worship is both a duty and a privilege for everyone who calls himself a Christian. We can even suggest that such attendance, loyal and devout yet critical of inadequacy, may be a way in which public worship will be improved in its quality and made more worthy of the God whom we worship.

Attendance is a duty, we have said. It is a duty because it is the necessary complement of personal prayer, preventing our praying from becoming idiosyncratic and individualistic. The writer of the Epistle to the Hebrews admonished his readers "not to forsake the assembling of yourselves together." He saw clearly that Christianity, like its ancestor Judaism, was in fact social in nature; he also saw, one may assume, although he did not say, that because Christians like everybody else are social beings, they need to be with their brethren in the faith—and more, it is their responsibility to be with them. A duty, but also a privilege—and a privilege because it enables each to share with all, to give to and receive from the fellowship, to make public profession of and witness to the faith that is ours and to encourage others to do so by sharing in a common activity.

Public worship in church has another significant

value. By ourselves, we are quite likely to stress, both in our praying and in our believing and action, those particular aspects of Christian faith and practice that have their special appeal to us as individuals. We need to have these supplemented by other aspects that are not so obviously appealing to us. Public worship does this. In it we are drawn with our brethren along a path that opens to us new vistas and new points of interest. The following of what sometimes is called "the Christian year" is an example. Christmas and the season of preparation that precedes it, the time of special penitence during Lent, Holy Week and above all Good Friday, Easter Day, the coming of the Holy Spirit on Pentecost: here is a regular round of observance that provides variety in such churches as observe it—and they are increasing in number, in all denominations. But above all, here is entrance into the "large room" of traditional Christian faith, delivering us from unhealthy confinement to personal preference and enlarging our awareness of the richness of the Christian reality to which we belong.

The use of ancient prayers in public worship unites us with our ancestors in the Christian way; modern prayers bring us into contact with the contemporary world and its needs, as well as with our brethren across the world in our own day. The varied lessons read in church from Old and New Testaments disclose the many different aspects of truth about God and man. Psalms give us a share in what has been styled "the hymnbook that Jesus himself used." Hymns and canticles of more recent composition, but also the old ones that have come down to us from our Christian past, enable us to sing the praises of God along with those who have gone before us, while they unite us with others present at worship in a common act of

adoration or petition or confession. And the sermon—
which we may hope will be no series of moral plati-
tudes or pious phrases, but a real proclamation of the
gospel of God in Christ—can be for us, as it is meant
always to be, the very Word of God brought to bear
upon our human lives.

Above all, public worship is the experience of
sharing with our fellow-Christians in an action that is
distinctively Christian and which, by our very presence there, is to become (like all prayer) an intentional, attentive, and conscious openness to the
presence and action of God himself. Thus we are
delivered from loneliness as Christian believers. We
know ourselves to be part of "a great company which
no man can number," for in such worship we enter
with full awareness into "the communion of saints"
and know ourselves to be "members of the blessed
company of all faithful people." This is an enormous
encouragement for us modern Christians, perhaps
more for us than for our ancestors in faith since
today Christian profession is not simply taken for
granted in the community and we can feel very much
alone in making that profession. "The world is too
much with us"; we are ever in danger of losing our
way or finding our faith dim. Being with other Christians in the public worship of God strengthens us,
confirms us in faith, and sends us out to our daily
tasks with renewed determination "to continue
Christ's faithful soldiers and servants unto our life's
end."

One additional comment may be made in this
connection. Those who are with us in church may not
be the ones with whom normally we should wish to
find ourselves. And that is all to the good. Participation in such worship has the advantage of bringing us,

Sunday by Sunday, into contact with "all sorts and conditions of men"; and we can learn in this way that God is "no respecter of persons" but welcomes *all* who turn to him, however unattractive or uninteresting or disagreeable they may seem to us to be. If God is willing to accept them, we can learn to accept them too. "Not many wise, not many noble"—just ordinary people, as doubtless they on their part think us to be. And all of them are our brethren, for whom we are to care and in whose presence we are to rejoice.

These days church attendance has fallen off a great deal. This may seem unfortunate, but it has *one* good aspect. Most of those who now "go to church" do so because they are convinced that Christian faith is true and important, or at least that it may have "something" to say and give to them. People do not come nowadays, so much as was once the case, simply in order to be "respectable"; indeed, in many places it is perfectly possible to be thus "respectable," to be good, decent citizens, without ever darkening the doors of a church.

We should not condemn people who at an earlier period went to church because that was what everybody did. Churchgoing is not likely to hurt anybody! The real question is what happens to them when they are there. But granted this, the ordinary believing Christian will find today that those who are with him in church will be, like him, concerned to grow in faith, to deepen their relationship with God, and to learn from public prayer ways in which their devotion, in private prayer and otherwise, may be given more reality. In such a situation, the duty and privilege of church worship is clear enough. Our Christian brethren need us; we need them.

In this chapter we have urged that praying in

church is no meaningless or incidental activity but is tied in with the whole of our Christian profession and our common humanity. It has to do with the whole man. "It is good for the brethren to dwell together in unity," the Psalm tells us. Above all, it is good and necessary for Christian people to pray together, as well as to pray privately, to come together regularly and faithfully in order to receive grace for daily living, to praise God, to thank him, to intercede before him, and to find in him their truest "joy and salvation."

6/
Praying at the Lord's Supper

From earliest days the Christian fellowship has celebrated the Lord's Supper as its greatest act of worship. We are told in Acts how the first Christians met "to break bread." And from that time to the present, the distinctive aspect of their worship, distinguishing them from other people in their religion, has been this continuing "memorial of the death of Christ." Only the Society of Friends, among regularly organized traditional Christian groups, has not observed this sacrament; yet for them, every meal together, they tell us, has the character of a holy communion. So too with the more recently founded Salvation Army.

As we shall see, this sacramental observance has its associations with Jewish worship. It also brings to fulfilment pagan sacred meals, accomplishing what they were unable to do although their intention was a communion of some sort with whatever divine power they worshipped. But the Christian sacrament is especially related to the life, death, and resurrection of Christ that it "recalls," as the phrase so often used tells us. It is the way in which the Lord who lived in

Palestine in the days of his flesh becomes a living presence, in all his genuine *presentness*, to his people. Not that it is the *only* way, of course, for in all our praying (and otherwise, too) he makes himself known; but in *this* way, he is known in a special and peculiarly intensive manner.

In some Christian churches, the Lord's Supper is the chief service every Sunday and is often celebrated on weekdays too. Luther and Calvin wished that on every Lord's Day there should be one great service, including sacrament and sermon. For various reasons, this desire was not realized; and only in recent years has there been a return, in many places, to more frequent observance of the Supper. Nonetheless, its centrality and importance have always been stressed and anyone who has attended the quarterly celebrations in, say, the Scottish Highlands can see how profoundly significant the Supper is even when only celebrated four times a year. During my own lifetime I have observed the way in which more and more Christian groups are holding the Holy Communion with increasing frequency; and surely this is all to the good. The day may yet come when in Reformed churches, as in Catholic ones, it will be a regular weekly action; thus the intention of Luther and Calvin will be fulfilled at last.

In this chapter we are to consider the ways in which Christian prayer is carried on and carried out at the *Eucharist*—from the Greek word for "Thanksgiving" which was the name given the sacrament in early Christian days. But before we do this, it will be well to say something more about the origins and earliest development of the rite. Often we are enabled to understand some practice by knowing how it came to be and how it has been understood in the past;

then we can interpret it for ourselves, in our own time.

It seems that during his days in Palestine Jesus held meals of table fellowship with his disciples and followers; the gospel stories of the so-called "feedings" would suggest this. But on the evening before his crucifixion and death, he gathered his friends with him in an "upper room" to join with him in a particular meal that recent scholarship implies was a regular Jewish observance. This meal always included conversation on matters of faith, but it found its climax in the breaking of bread before the repast proper and the sharing of a common cup when it was finished. We even know the words Jesus probably said in "blessing" the bread and wine. Jewish "blessings" were in the form of thanksgiving addressed to God; and the appropriate words on that occasion would have been something like this: "Blessed be thou, Lord God of the universe, who hast given bread for man's sustenance. . . . Blessed be thou, Lord God of the universe, who hast given wine for man's rejoicing in heart."

But because on that occasion the Jewish Feast of the Passover was at hand, there must have been some note of that festival in the meal. The Jewish Passover is the recalling of God's deliverance of his people from the Egyptians; it is a feast remembering God as the savior of the Jews. Just how this played its part in the Last Supper we do not know, and the experts have different theories about the matter. Yet in some way Jesus' reference, in breaking and distributing the bread and in giving the cup, seems to point to his intention of indicating the significance of his approaching death as well as entering into fellowship with his friends. He said, "This my body broken for you. . . . This cup the new covenant in my blood, shed for you," or some variant of these words. This is the historical beginning of the Lord's Supper. Jesus evidently meant to make his disciples sharers, there and then, in the new relationship with God that his own body broken and his own blood shed would establish for men. And every time they "remembered" him, by doing at their fellowship meals what he had done on that last occasion, they would find him present with them, until his "coming again."

With the resurrection of the Lord, the disciples were assured that he was still with them, victorious over all that had brought him to his death; and as they met for those continuing meals of fellowship they found him "in the breaking of the bread." His promise had been fulfilled. They experienced the joy of the Kingdom, whose coming was anticipated in the meal; as they ate the bread and drank of the cup they were already with the risen Lord who would come again to them and to all men. Throughout Christian history, this has been experienced again and again. Christians have had the same sense of his presence, the same certainty of his living reality, the same joy in being inheritors of the Kingdom of God—all made known and assured to them as they have gathered at the Lord's Table and have done what Jesus commanded men to do in his "remembrance."

Of course the way in which the sacrament has been understood has developed from the early days; of course the manner of its celebration has changed greatly over the years. But it is the same action, whether it be conducted elaborately, with great splendor, color, lights, and music, or very simply and plainly. Both ways of doing it are appropriate—the simple ones because often the significance of an action is best known in stark simplicity, the elaborate ones because it is natural for men to wish to surround a treasured occasion with as much dignity as they can manage. In whatever way it is done, it remains what Thomas Aquinas once finely called it, "the summing up of the whole mystery of our salvation." All Christians, Catholic and Reformed, Evangelical and whatever else, would agree with him.

A service like this can have many meanings, not all of them immediately obvious to the occasional attendant. We shall now consider some of these meanings, which will suggest to us ways in which we may most effectively pray at the Holy Communion. But first of all we must insist on the fact that we have to do here with an *action*, with something that is *done*. That is of enormous importance for our proper grasp of its significance.

The Lord's Supper includes words, since its meaning must be expressed. But it is not fundamentally a form of words, any more than it is a set of pious thoughts in which Christians unite. In the gospel narratives of the Last Supper Jesus is reported to have said, "*Do* this in my remembrance," not *think* this or *say* this. He was performing an action in which others were to engage. They were not just to say things to one another nor by mental reverie remember (in our *modern* sense) events in the past. They were to take bread and wine, do things with them and share them. Any speaking or thinking would be the consequence of this doing. We shall say more about the kind of remembrance here in view when we come to the "memorial aspect" of the Eucharist.

First, then, the action is an action of the Christian

community; it is a social matter. That is why it is so important that Christians should be present at it, as a family of faithful men and women. Here in this social act is the expression of a common allegiance to Christ and the reality of a common sharing in his life and what he has done—his "benefits," as theologians would say. We may not feel particularly "pious" at the sacrament; this will be largely a matter of our temperament. But that does not matter, since it is not our feelings but our presence, with the right intentions, that counts most. We shall know ourselves unworthy; but this is food for *sinners*, not for saints already made perfect. Dr. James Stewart has told of an old Scots minister who said to a girl who held back from receiving the bread because she felt her great unworthiness, "Take it, lass, it's *meant* for sinners!"

In the second place, the Lord's Supper is an expression of Christian joy in accepting what Christ has done for men. An old phrase used to describe it is, "This our sacrifice of praise and thanksgiving." We are there to thank God for the redemption of the world by our Lord Jesus Christ. That redemption was wrought through his suffering and death, to be sure; but he is risen in triumph, his deed done, his work confirmed when "God raised him from the dead." How can a Christian fail to rejoice? How can he be other than glad for so great a redemption, now "shown forth" in the sacred meal? Here is our opportunity to give praise, adoration, and thanks to God, in company with our Christian brethren, as we know Christ's presentness with us, his victory for us, and his assurance of continuing grace given to us, sinful men though we are.

Third, the sacrament is the "remembrance" of Christ. But we must be careful lest we use this word

in its modern sense, where it suggests our turning
back simply in thought to events in the past. The
Hebrew idea was very different—and it still is different. When the ancient Jews (and modern ones too)
engage in their Passover, they do not regard this as a
memory in our modern sense; rather, it is for them an
action—sharing a meal, telling a story, doing certain
things—that makes present for them in the here and
now what they believe God did for them when he
delivered them from the Egyptians and led them
safely into the promised land. The memorial is thus a
vital recalling of the past into the present, so that it
becomes a reality in which they now genuinely share.

So, too, in the Christian memorial or remembrance
of the death and resurrection of Jesus Christ. Many
know the Negro spiritual, "Were you there when they
crucified my Lord?" When the believer is at the
Lord's Supper he is sure that he *is* present at the
crucifixion—and at the resurrection too. Here Christ's
presentness, in all that he was and did, in all that he
still is and does, is known. Thus in the Church's
sacramental remembrance there is a living presence,
not a dead reverie or a merely mental recollection.

In the fourth place, the Christ who is thus remembered is the Christ whose death was a sacrifice for
men. That death must be seen in the context of his
whole life, for *tota vita Christi mysterium crucis*, as a
medieval saying has it: "the whole life of Christ is the
mystery of the Cross." All of his life was an offering
of himself to what he knew to be the will of the
Father; it was summed up on Calvary when he "was
obedient unto death, even the death of the Cross."
When at the Eucharist Christian people remember
Christ, his sacrificial life and death are there with
them. They are incorporated into that perfect offer-

ing and empowered, in their own small degree, also to
offer themselves a "living sacrifice, acceptable to
God." What William Law, an old English writer, once
called "the process of Christ" is to be worked out in
them: they, too, are to know obedience, sacrifice,
death, and resurrection. And in consequence they
become "other Christs" to their brethren in the
world, as Benedict in the early Church and Martin
Luther in the sixteenth century were bold enough to
affirm.

How all these things are accomplished we do not
know. There have been many theories, all of them
speculative and most of them elaborations from
philosophical or theological ideas popular at a particular time and place. If we are to have any theory at
all, maybe we should accept them *all*, trying to find
some truth in what they are saying! But it is best to
have *no* theory—or at least, not to set up any ex-
clusive theory or set of theories about how Christ is
at the Eucharist, what is going on in detail, and the
like. Some of us would be content simply to use the
words of an Elizabethan English rhyme:

> He was the Word that spake it;
> He took the bread and brake it.
> And what his word did make it
> *That* I believe and take it.

This is a reverent agnosticism about the *how*, refusing
to speculate overmuch about the rite but rejoicing in
Christ as a present reality known in the sacrament.

For Christian devotion, surely, it is sufficient to
know that Christ comes to those who believe in him.
It is sufficient to know that he is truly *there* by the
instrumentality of bread and wine taken, blessed, and
shared. His people feed on him in their hearts, by

faith, with thanksgiving. Need we say more? God was in Christ, but no man can say exactly how this could be. Christ's presentness is in the sacrament; and again no man can explain just how this is possible. We need not try to exceed our limited human capacity for knowing.

For the Christian who wishes to learn to pray, no better occasion is given than at the Lord's Table, for the Holy Communion *is* Christian prayer in a supreme mode. For one thing, it is a means of fellowship with God and with our brethren. It is fellowship with our brethren, since Christ is both the Brother of all men and the "Head" of the human race. He is Man as man is meant to be; and each of us can find in him the pattern of manhood. But in him, as Man, God was actively present, incarnate among us. Thus there is fellowship with God. If the purpose of prayer is such a communion with God, by identification with him in our desires and willing, here is the accomplished fact, once for all effected in history.

Here, too, is opportunity for confession of sin and the receiving of God's pardon, for prayer for ourselves and for others, for thanksgiving to God, and for sheer adoration. In other words, all the elements of prayer, as we have described them, are gathered up and given new and vitalizing expression.

Several times we have used the word "Eucharist" as the name for the sacrament; we pointed out that it is the Greek word for "Thanksgiving" and was employed regularly for the service in the early days of the Christian Church. It is appropriate to take that word and apply it to the Christian himself: *he* is to be a "living eucharist," a living thanksgiving to God for all that God has done, now does, and will do. At the service itself, this becomes clear. And when the believer leaves the church building and goes out into the world, his life of thanksgiving is to continue unchanged. What happens *after* the sacrament is a demonstration of what takes place *during* it.

So it is that on weekdays, in office or store or school or home or factory, the Christian is the eucharistic man, living in thankfulness to God and showing his thankfulness in all that he says and does. He is a placarding of Christ before men. Perhaps he is not an especially notable person, but he has the root of the matter in him. His daily private prayer, his public worship, and above all his participation in the Lord's Supper, Holy Communion, or Eucharist, now find outward manifestation in "the works of love," wherever he may be. They used to say of the first Christians that "men took notice of them, that they had been with Jesus." So it should be with modern Christians too—and the place, opportunity, and occasion to be "with Jesus" in a very special way is at the sacrament.

It may be well to conclude this chapter with some practical hints. Here they are:

(1) Attend the Lord's Supper regularly and faithfully, however difficult it may be to get to it and however dim one's devotion may seem at the time.

(2) Receive the sacramental elements as often as you can, whenever opportunity offers—perhaps your congregation could be persuaded to make it available more frequently.

(3) Do not look for special thrills or "shivers up your back," as an old friend once put it. The purpose of the sacrament is not to stir our emotions so much as to enable us to grow in Christ, to the "measure of the stature" of his manhood and as faithful children of God who is our Father.

(4) Prepare for the service, simply and without any fuss; and afterwards give thanks for it, equally simply and without fuss.

(5) Remember afterward that you have "been with Jesus"; and try to carry out in your daily life what you have seen, known, and received.

Thus you will find yourself growing in prayer and you will know the joy of Christian living.

7 / Making Prayer Meaningful Today

This has been a book about prayer, intended for modern men and women who find difficulty not only in seeing how prayer is possible but in understanding what it really is. We have defined prayer as the intentional and attentive presence of God, with the purpose of alignment of self—in desires and actions—with the divine Lover who is our heavenly Father. We have set prayer in the context of the Christian faith that God *is* Love as revealed in Jesus Christ; and we have sought to take account of modern knowledge of the world so that prayer does not seem an unreal escape from the facts that we all know about that world. And we have looked at various aspects of prayer—in word, in thought, in public worship, at the Lord's Supper. Through all of these occasions opportunity is given us to open ourselves to God, to link our little manhood with his divine will, and to cooperate with God as his "fellow-workers," in the word used by Paul.

As we have shown, prayer is to a large degree a matter of *attention;* we quoted a classical definition that said that "prayer is the attentive presence of

God." Of course we are *always* in God's presence; it is like the air we breathe. But like the air, it is not always vividly realized as being there. We must make a conscious effort if the presence is to be known to us at first hand and not simply by hearsay. Yet "effort" may be the wrong word, since it could suggest that prayer is just a business of struggle, striving, almost of combat. This is not really the case; although there must be determination and concentration in prayer, there is also "resting in prayer" (as our fathers in the faith used to say), and delight and refreshment for us as we engage in it.

We have also looked at some of the problems posed to modern people, but we have seen that most of these are reflections of mistaken ideas, theologically and scientifically as well as philosophically and practically. Once we have got the right perspective, most of these problems take care of themselves. At the same time we have recognized that for modern people there are certain questions that require a rather different emphasis in our praying from that of former days. How to pray, how to arrange occasions and opportunities of prayer, and the types of prayer may not be the same as for an earlier period of Christian history. We have discussed "vocal" prayer, as it has been called, in its various aspects; we have also discussed "mental" prayer, laying particular stress on the simplicity of meditation and the desirability of engaging in it. Then we have looked at public prayer, saying a great deal about its congruity with human nature and human life and attempting to show that it is both a duty and a privilege for anyone who would call himself a Christian in any serious sense of the term. Finally, we have considered eucharistic prayer at the Lord's Supper, as the focal point for all Christian praying and the center of Christianity as such, urging that it should also be the focus and center of the life of prayer of every Christian believer.

In this closing chapter we shall try to relate all this to the Christian enterprise in its totality. After all, unless prayer "fits in" and thus both makes sense of and gives sense to that enterprise, it may appear as no more than a peripheral although useful exercise in the life of Christian discipleship. But it *does* "fit in"; and precisely for this reason it is what Montgomery called it in the hymn quoted at the beginning, "the Christian's vital breath."

Perhaps our best approach here will be to consider the plain fact that the world in which we live presents itself to us as a *mystery*. Now a mystery is to be sharply distinguished from a *problem*. The French thinker Gabriel Marcel has pointed out that a problem is something with which we can deal; we can "solve" it. Of course we may not be able to do this immediately; perhaps we may not be in a position to make much progress toward its solution. But *in principle*, when we are given a problem, we know that there is a genuine possibility of its solution. A mystery, on the other hand, is very different. A mystery is that which puts us in awe; we cannot "solve" it, we can only accept it and wonder at it. Bertrand Russell was an excellent example of the sort of man who honestly recognized mystery when he saw it. Despite his agnostic position in respect to religious faith, Russell had no patience with what he called "cosmic impiety," by which he meant the assumption that somehow by manipulation and techniques the mysterious puzzle of the universe could be neatly solved and everything made tidy. He criticized the American philosopher John Dewey on precisely this ground.

The mystery in things is spoken to each of us. Some contemporary writers have pretended that modern people do not acknowledge that there is any mystery at all. One can only wonder how well they know those about whom they write. Within the weeks during which this book has been written, I have seen the reality of the sense of mystery time and again in people whom I have met. For example, there was the young couple so deeply in love. They were waiting for a bus, simply standing on the pavement at a bus stop. But to witness the wonder that was in their eyes as they looked at each another and murmured I do not know what, was to see the great mystery of love. No amount of physiological, psychological, sociological, or any other type of problem-solving would have eradicated that mystery. Or again, when I began this book I was sitting with friends on the terrace of a resort hotel, with the stars brilliant in the sky, with the hush of late evening around us. I noticed that the littleness of man against the background of the "infinite spaces" (as Pascal phrased it in his *Pensées*) made its impression upon them. Oddly enough, it was just after the first landing of men on the moon; yet that great achievement had not obliterated the mystery of the vast expanse of the heavens above us.

Two other examples brought this sense of mystery, as felt by ordinary people, vividly home to me. I was listening with others to a superb rendition of the Third Symphony of Beethoven (the *Eroica*). There was silence, so pregnant that one could feel its presence—and at the very end, before the applause broke out, there was another silence, a strange testimony to the fact that here, in great music greatly performed, a mysterious quality had impinged on those who heard.

And finally, a very simple thing indeed: two young people, standing with their newly born baby held by the mother. Sheer wonder was in their eyes as they looked at this tiny bit of humanity, brought into existence by their own sexual union, yet obviously speaking to them of the wonderful and mysterious creation of an entirely new life.

We are surrounded by mystery and we live in mystery; and the day when the awareness of it vanishes will be the day when man is no longer man, for he will have lost his capacity to grow, to love, to wonder, to yearn for some strange "more" that beckons to him and speaks to him in all his experience. But that day will never come. And my reason for thinking this includes, among other things, the fact that my scientific friends in a great college of a great university (among them many agnostics and self-identified "atheists") are the very people who often seem to me *most* aware of mystery in the world, even in the scientific research that they carry on with such devotion and yet with such humility.

But if we know that the world presents us with mystery, we also believe that it has a *meaning*. The meaning may be obscure, but some sense of the significance of things is an integral element in human life. Even a professed atheist like Jean-Paul Sartre, despite his protests and despite his insistence that the only meaning is what we ourselves put into things, evidently still finds sufficient sense in the simple fact of living so that he does not take his own life. Schubert Ogden has writen an essay on "The Strange Witness of Unbelief" (included in his book *The Reality of God*, SCM Press, London, 1967), in which he demonstrates how often it is the very negators of meaning whose way of life, attitude toward others, and struggle for a "better world" exhibit a dim yet pervasive feeling of significance in the world and in their own existence, a sense of meaning that (as Ogden argues and as I believe) is a hidden working of divine Love in their hearts.

Meaning, then, is universally sought and universally presupposed. We speak of the universe as a cosmos, not a chaos; we believe that we are in touch with how things go in the world, so that we can to some degree understand them; we count on regularity, predictability, orderliness, as present and real—and what are all these but a mute testimony to *meaning?* But underneath the obvious "meanings" of the immediate facts that we encounter, we are led to ask the question about "ultimate" or "final" meaning. Does the whole enterprise, in its mystery and with its problems, *mean* anything? What is its *true* significance? Man is a *meaning-giving* animal; can it be that he is also an animal who is *found by* meaning—meaning that illuminates his darkness and gives dignity and purpose to his little day in this vast world?

Where do we find meaning spoken to us? Usually, I think, in the very places where we sense mystery. In the joy of human companionship, in the call of duty, in the sense of awe on a starry night, in the face of the one for whom we care, in great music, in beauty, in the presence of courage—here are some of the places. But above all we find meaning speaking to us in the pathos of our human loving—and I have said *pathos* because I intend here combined joy and sadness, the awareness of another with whom we would unite our lives yet the equal awareness that the other, even when he also would unite his life with ours, remains "the other" whom we must reverence for himself. This distinctively human experience of love, its commitment of self, its giving of self, its readiness to receive the other's gift of self, its evocation of hope, and its capacity to fulfil, is not something that just "happens to us." The world is the sort of world where this can be known; and in knowing it we are released and empowered. Meaning comes to us at such times; and when it comes it gives us dignity as men and women.

It is in such a context, I believe, that religion at its truest and best is crucial to man. In primitive days men were aware of an emptiness that had to be filled with innumerable divine powers working in ordinary things. Later, or even at the same time, life was marked by a dreadful fear of such powers. The divine was seen as man's enemy who must be placated if harm were to be avoided. But when religion was rationalized and moralized, in the light of man's own growing sense of order and his increasing awareness that mutuality and love were the condition of human community, it became more and more a sense that the worth in things, the significance they possessed, the meaning they had, could be found only in love and in loving. This process of development is seen in all parts of the world, as for example in India and in China, so very different one from the other yet moving toward compassion as the key to life (in India) or family affection and mutual concern in an ordered society as that key (as in China).

The Jewish religious experience, from earliest days through its highest moments in a Jeremiah and an Isaiah, is also a development from primitive fear of omnipotent power to communion with a goodness that seeks only the best for men. Thus when Jesus appeared, his coming was against that background. What the event of Christ accomplished was the purifi-

cation of ancient Jewish insight and the completion
of ancient Jewish aspiration; in him Love was seen at
work in a fashion that those who responded knew to
be both mysterious and full of meaning in their lives.
That Love, humanly expressed to the point of sacrificial death, was validated and confirmed, for Christian faith, in the resurrection of embodied Love from
death and hatred, evil and deception. *God* was like
that; indeed God *was* that Love, only he was its
source and its goal—the human love of Jesus was the
expression in terms of genuine human existence of
"the Love that moves the sun and the other stars."
God as Love and man with his human loving were not
identical, since God is transcendent over the creation—he is unexhausted by what he does there, he is
ceaselessly faithful, he is supreme and altogether excellent. Yet in human loving, such as Jesus disclosed,
the divine Love was shared and outpoured.

So Jesus is that One in whom the deepest and
highest reality, divine Love, which is the mystery
behind all things and the meaning of all things, is
made decisively visible and tangible in a manhood
that is our own and in terms that we can understand
and grasp, and by which we can be grasped and thus
directed on the path of right and true human development. This is Christian faith—nothing other, nothing
less. The meaning of the mystery is Love; and it is the
only meaning as it is the enduring survival from what
goes on in a world of "perishing occasions."

What we have been saying about prayer and its
practice has this broader context. It is man's desire to
work with the purpose of Love and it is his opening
of himself to that working. All the magical notions
about prayer as the conforming of things to one's
own imperfect notions fade away. Most of the prob-

lems that have been raised about prayer are shown to be based on a misunderstanding of what prayer *really* is. Modern men and women can pray with just as much sincerity, honesty, and devotion as could their ancestors in the Christian tradition. And they can pray with their whole selves, disregarding the nonsense that has been talked about prayer as a matter of merely "spiritual" nature. Indeed, *any* man who knows what it is to love and be loved can pray— Christian faith does not contradict the meaning of his praying, but crowns it and fulfils it, while correcting inadequate and childish ideas about what that praying intends.

Some readers may think that the constant emphasis in this book on love, on God as Love, on man as being created for love, and on love as the deepest significance of prayer, has been overdone. He may think so; but I believe that he is terribly and tragically mistaken. It has already been made clear that by love we have not meant sentimentality or niceness or indifference or kind toleration. It is very difficult to eradicate from many minds the notion that this is always what one means so soon as the word "love" is uttered. Yet to entertain that notion is to show oneself imperceptive as well as inattentive. Love is a very terrible reality, precisely because it is a glorious one. There is nothing soft or weak about genuine love. It is "terrible as an army with banners," in the Old Testament phrase. It is the only *really* strong thing in the world, because it is what Paul said it is: never failing, able to endure all things and yet still *be* love. God is that; and even human love, in all its frustration and distortion, can touch such heights now and again.

Furthermore, love is *passionate*. Here again there are some who would not agree. They think of passionate love, perhaps after the fashion suggested by Dr. Anders Nygren in his well-known book *Agape and Eros*, as selfish in desiring a response and damaging in its feeling-tones of high intensity. Hence they reject it as an inappropriate term for man's relation to God and substitute "faith" instead. For them "faith" is a steady setting of the will on God in commitment or surrender; and the only kind of love that is truly "religious" is the intent of the *will* on another's good. I believe that this analysis is biblically mistaken, historically false, theologically disastrous, and psychologically impossible. *All* love, even in the somewhat chilly sense of this "faith-love," has an element of passion. This means that it contains some genuine *desire*, perhaps not strongly felt but nonetheless present. If that element of desire were not there, it is hard to see how anyone could be "moved" to love, as we commonly say. We could observe and even sympathize in an external way; but we could not urgently identify ourselves with the condition, the problems, the suffering, as well as the joy, of other people. "Cold charity" would be all we could manage; and that is a quite dreadful thing for the recipient, even if it may for a moment assuage his need and provide him with food and clothing.

But *Christian* love is not "cold charity"; it is charity with a passionate concern for others and a deeply felt care for their situation. This is what makes all the difference in the world between the well-intentioned and zealous social worker, good and important as such a person is, and the man or woman who gives *himself* to a needy and hungry and lonely person. The old saying tells us that "the gift without the giver is bare"—and I am convinced that one reason that aid programs so often meet with antagonism even from those who most will benefit from them is explained in just this way. Perhaps an incident from my own experience will illustrate my meaning. Many years ago a black student of mine was in great trouble. He came to see me to talk over the problem he faced. I made what suggestions I could and at the end of the half-hour walked with him to the door of my study. As we approached the door, I put my hand on his shoulder and spoke some words of encouragement. To my horror, the young man broke into tears. Thinking that what I had said might have offended him, I apologized. And then that young black student said this: "You can't understand why I'm crying, try as hard as you will." I answered, "Well, tell me why and I'll attempt to understand." He said, "I'm crying because you're the first white man who has ever *touched* me." Then he fled from the room. And *I* wept. I wept because I had been made to see, for the first time, that all the justice that must be shown the black man, all the help given him, everything that should be done legally to give him his rights, will never do what a simple act of love can do: make him know that he is accepted, cared for, yes, really loved by those who do not just "do good to him" but who *feel* with passionate concern that he is a human brother.

I apologize for this bit of personal biography; but at least it makes my point. Love *does* involve feeling; at its best it *is* passionate. Now this is why I have ventured to stress the sexual component in human nature and to urge that it be brought into our praying. Our sexuality is the physiological-psychological basis for desire—that is, for passion. The Beatles had a song in which they said,

For she loves you, and you know that can't be bad;
She loves you, and you know you should be glad.

In their singing of it, the lines obviously and intentionally had specifically sexual or erotic overtones.
But why not? There *is* a sexual element in all love—
even, I should wish to urge, in all friendship and
indeed in all human relationships that are not external or superficial. Man is a unity and his sexuality is
integral to that unity. What is more, for most human
beings it is precisely when they begin to see that
someone loves them, whether this is in an explicitly
sexual sense or not, that they discover their capacity
to be truly alive and to grow toward genuine fulfilment as persons designed to become lovers of God
and men.

I am sure that only those who have come to some
such awakening, because they have been deeply loved
and because in some strange fashion they have been
enabled to love in return, can ever understand what
Christian prayer is really about. Augustine's saying,
"He who has loved will know what I mean," had
reference to his theological insistence that God always comes first to men and through his coming
arouses them to respond to him. But what he said is
equally applicable to our praying. Among the many
reasons for living, so far as we can, in relationships of
active love with others, is this: that we can then begin
to pray, and keep on praying, with sincerity and
dedication and with some genuine grasp of what
prayer means.

For as we have stressed throughout this book, the
purpose of prayer is to bring God's human child, now
become adult in responsibility and thus asked to act
in mature ways, into cooperative awareness of God,

opened to his love and ready to act in love toward others. But we can now see why it is necessary to go on to say that a consequence of prayer, when it is faithfully and regularly engaged in, will be the release of the praying person from bondage to cheapness and superficiality, from slavery to immediate instinct and unworthy desire, into "the glorious liberty of the children of God." What *is* that liberty? Surely it is growing ability to love, growing willingness to accept love as offered to us, increasing delight in giving ourselves to others who in their turn give themselves to us. That is the human consequence. As to the divine consequence, it is the growing awareness of a cosmic Love, a cosmic Lover, that holds us tight, that never lets us go, that stays with us in all our problems and troubles and sufferings as well as in our joys and delights, that lives with us and for us, and that in the end receives us into his own life—where we are forever loved in the Love that endures, beyond all "changes and chances," in the everlastingness that is God himself.